THE RACING WORLD

JULIAN WILSON

THE RACING WORLD

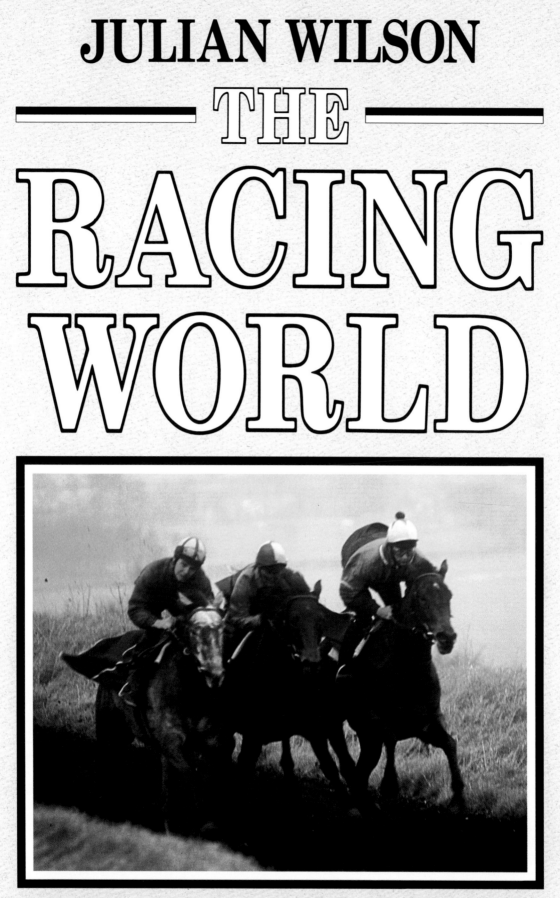

PHOTOGRAPHS BY JORGE LEWINSKI

Macdonald Queen Anne Press

A QUEEN ANNE PRESS BOOK

© Text: Julian Wilson 1991
© Photographs: Jorge Lewinski 1991

First published in Great Britain in 1991 by
Queen Anne Press, a division of
Macdonald & Co (Publishers) Ltd
165 Great Dover Street
London SE1 4YA

A member of the Maxwell Macmillan Pergamon Publishing Corporation

Design: Peter Champion and Michael Harris

A CIP catalogue record for this book is available from the British Library

ISBN 0-356-18655-5

Typeset by Tradespools Ltd, Frome, Somerset

Printed in Great Britain by BPCC Hazell Books, Paulton and Aylesbury
Member of BPCC Ltd

Contents

Photographer's Acknowledgements 6

Flat Racing

Introduction 10

The Owner-Breeder *Bill Gredley* 14

The Stud Groom *Michael Thomas* 26

The Vet *Nick Wingfield-Digby* 39

The Bloodstock Agent *John Warren* 52

The Auctioneer *Richard Mildmay-White* 61

The Trainer *Ian Balding* 75

The Head Lad *Bill Palmer* 96

The Stable Lad *John Wilkinson* 107

The Jockey *Steve Cauthen* 116

National Hunt

Introduction 132

The Trainer *Gordon W. Richards* 135

The Jump Jockey *Neale Doughty* 159

Photographer's Acknowledgements

Firstly I would like to extend my warmest thanks to a number of important personalities of the racing world who gave me their unstinting support, as well as their precious time. It would not have been possible to complete this book without their help.

Ian Balding and Gordon W. Richards were particularly generous and co-operative, and in their stables, paddocks and gallops I spent many happy hours. Ian Balding even went as far as arranging special gallops, late in the season, to allow me to shoot last-minute photographs for this book. My thanks are also due to Stetchworth Park Stud and its owner Bill Gredley who virtually gave me the run of the place. His stud groom Michael Thomas (who is no longer there) was especially helpful in alerting me to crucial moments in the life of the stud. His middle-of-the-night telephone call got me out of bed barely half an hour before the birth of Diana's Bow's son. But in fact every single individual featured in this book went out of his or her way to afford me assistance and advice. I shadowed Nick Wingfield-Digby for a whole day on his rounds around Newmarket stables and my camera was allowed to sneak a look at some of his more onerous duties, including surgical operations and x-raying some ailing horses. Both John Warren, with his charming wife Lady Carolyn Warren, and Richard Mildmay-White agreed to additional photographic sessions. Our two 'star' jockeys, Neale Doughty and Steve Cauthen, were equally generous with their time and assistance.

Readers of this book will perhaps be interested in some of the problems and techniques involved in its production.

When I was commissioned to work on *The Racing World* I contacted my good friend Harry Collins, the managing director of Nikon Ltd. He immediately suggested that I should photograph the whole book with their, at the time, new camera – the Nikon F801 – since it would be most suited to the task ahead of me. The choice could not have been better.

With some thirty years' experience behind me, I, like many seasoned professional photographers, have always been slightly mistrustful of the modern trend towards sophisticated automation in cameras. I still tend, as often as not, to take my light readings with a hand exposure meter, and auto-focus seemed to me to be an unnecessary refinement. But quite frankly the F801 has converted me.

Its 'matrix' exposure metering, which divides the image seen through the viewfinder into five segments and computerises them into no less than 25 'matrix' boxes to provide the best possible exposure in various situations, proved to be remarkably accurate. Only in the most extreme cases, for example when shooting into the light, did I have to resort to a hand meter.

As one would expect, the overwhelming majority of photographs in this book are of horses or people with horses, and most of these were impossible to stage or set up in any way. Most of the time I had to shoot off the cuff. It is in these kinds of situations that reliable built-in exposure calculation and automatic focusing are invaluable. With very rapid auto-focus, if necessary with the camera set on 'continuous focus' to keep a fast-moving horse in sharp focus, and with the extremely useful 'black spot' in the viewfinder constantly confirming the spot-on focus, I was able to follow any action or change in the situation.

Those photographers who have never owned a fully dedicated-to-the-camera flashgun (in my case a superb SB24) do not know what they are missing. Dedicated flash not only picks up automatically the speed (ASA) of the film in the camera and the lens used, but it also allows for instantaneous change from full power to a 'fill-in' flash, which measures accurately the prevailing background light and adds any required additional light to provide a totally natural appearance of the image.

All in all, I have never before worked with a more versatile, reliable and friendly camera. It made my task so much easier and more enjoyable.

JORGE LEWINSKI

Flat Racing

Introduction

Horseracing is one of the most divisive, disparate industries of the modern world. Many years ago it was a sport, pure and simple. It was the exclusive leisure pursuit of the landed gentry, who employed training grooms and liveried riders to tend the horses as an extension of the estate workforce. Matches were made, private wagers struck, and fortunes won and lost. Most of the horses were home-bred, and the racing public received little or no valid information about either probable runners or the condition of horses. Touts – that dying breed who would hide in hedgerows to espy dawn gallops – were either horse-whipped or peppered with buckshot if apprehended, and ante-post betting on the great races was conducted at call-overs at the Victoria Club in London. Racing was aptly named 'The Sport of Kings'.

Racing in the 1990s is a horse of a very different colour. It is no longer a sport. It is a multi-million pound, labour-intensive industry. Racing and breeding have an annual turnover of millions. Betting has a turnover of billions. The two dominant bodies in horseracing are the Jockey Club, a self-electing oligarchy responsible for rules, discipline and administration, and the Horserace Betting Levy Board, a Government-appointed body in charge of racing's finances. The Levy Board was established when off-course betting – ie, betting shops – were made legal in 1961. Before that enactment, off-course cash betting was conducted by post with Scottish bookmakers; with an illegal street-corner bookie's runner; or, in Glasgow, in one of 600 illegal betting shops. The only legitimate means of cash betting on British racing was a visit to the races.

In the post-war era racing flourished. Money was plentiful; few individuals owned a television set and, in any case, outside broadcasts were in their infancy. There were over 100,000 racegoers at Newcastle on Pitmen's Derby Day, 1946. Racing, and in particular the racecourses, was thriving. Sadly for racing, neither the sport nor the Totalisator capitalised on those golden years. By the 1960s, attendances were falling away, television had become a major counter-attraction, and a growing lobby pressurised Government to legalise off-course betting and rid the factories and working men's clubs of the street-corner bookmaker. Thus the betting shop – alias 'gold mine' and 'a licence to print money' – was created, and the Levy Board established to compensate the racecourses in particular, and the industry in general, for the inevitable loss of revenue through the turnstiles.

In the subsequent 30 years, the off-course bookmakers have transformed themselves into billion-pound public companies, while the sport itself has

Dawn at Kingsclere. Trainer Ian Balding's first lot circle in Indian file on the Hollowshot work ground.

become under-financed to the extent that less than ten per cent of those professionally involved can earn a reasonable living. It is frequently expressed that 'the racing industry should get its act together, and present its case with a united front to Government'. Here lies the rub; racing will never present a united front. The Horserace Advisory Council, racing's consultative body created in 1980, is a multi-tentacled monster with almost every limb pulling in a different direction. Its General Council contains nominees from associations representing the racehorse owners, racecourses, breeders, trainers, jockeys, stable staff, racegoers, permit trainers, bloodstock agents, racehorse transporters, veterinary surgeons, Jockey Club officials, point-to-point owners, amateur riders, lady jockeys, and the TGWU. Try getting *that* lot to agree on any one subject – except that racing is under-financed! Almost all of these, together with blacksmiths, caterers, gatemen, journalists and photographers, earn their living from horseracing. So who makes a reasonable profit from the racing industry?

Owners

Owners are the ultimate underwriters. Training costs for a horse at Newmarket range from £10,000 to £15,000 per annum. On the flat, 8000 runners will be competing for just £25 million prize money in 1992. So the average horse recovers barely 25 per cent of his training costs. The more you own, the more you lose! But a good horse can hit the jackpot. A Derby winner will be syndicated for stud at a valuation of up to £10 million. This is the ultimate dream that keeps 8000 owners in pursuit of the crock of gold.

Trainers

Trainers represent an interesting cross-section of racing society. Traditionally they were training grooms, ex-jockeys, or the descendants of professional racing dynasties like the Waughs, Jarvises, Leaders and Watts in Newmarket. Nowadays, they come from family backgrounds in industry, commerce and even the landed gentry. A glance at the list of leading flat-race trainers reveals that many are associated with either titles or wealth. Henry Cecil, Roger Charlton, John Dunlop, Alex Scott, Alec Stewart and Peter Walwyn are all 'gentlemen trainers'. Sir Mark Prescott is a baronet, and William Hastings-Bass inherited the Earldom of Huntingdon last autumn.

What they have in common with the old-fashioned nagsman trainer is that almost all, except the top 20 trainers, struggle to make a living. Overheads like computers, facsimile machines, telephones, satellite TV, office staff, Mercedes cars, car telephones, champagne, laboratories, covered rides and building programmes, not to mention the property tax and providing accommodation for stable employees, make profit margins indiscernible. A Newmarket trainer who wins his patrons less than £400,000 a year (of which he earns ten per cent) is in danger of forfeiting his annual holiday in Barbados.

Jockeys

The top jockeys are the biggest earners in racing, outside of the big bookmaking chains. Pat Eddery and Willie Carson had contracts in 1990 rumoured to guarantee them a minimum income of £1 million. Steve Cauthen has a similarly enviable retainer. The top ten riders earn a very substantial income indeed. The top 30 are very comfortable. The unfashionable lightweights travel up to 400 miles for one ride, and would be better rewarded by working in a factory. Many end up doing so.

Breeders

Commercial breeders had a purple patch in the early 1980s, when yearling prices went through the ceiling. For the past four years, however, trade has gradually deteriorated, to the extent that, unless a breeder sells a foal or yearling to a Middle Eastern buyer, he is assured of another non-profitable year. Like the racehorse owner, however, the breeder soldiers on, borrowing more and more money, with the impossible dream of that 'One Good Horse'.

Bookmakers

When betting offices became legal in 1961, the old-established bookmaking firm of Ladbrokes had been in the hands of the Parker/Stein family for five years. Max Parker paid £250,000 for the business and the dynamic Cyril Stein swept into the original offices at 6, Old Burlington Street in June 1956. For the first three years under the new management Ladbrokes failed to make a profit. There was speculation that a bad result in the 1961 Derby would cause the firm to go bankrupt. Now, 30 years later, the Ladbroke Group is a multinational corporation with Group profits in 1990, before tax, of £305.6 million. The Racing Division earned £91.7 million. Ladbrokes reckon to corner around 25 per cent of the betting market. The profits achieved by successful betting shop management have helped build a number of financial empires.

Racing's yield from the Levy, meanwhile, hovers wearily around £40 million, whilst trainers go to the wall, stable employees live on the breadline, and breeders leave their mares empty rather than pay unviable nomination fees to stallion owners. Yet the racing game retains a unique, hypnotic magic. Owners who have said 'Never again' cannot resist the lure of the yearling sales. Trainers decide to give it 'one more year'. Breeders buy a new mare with the dream of a Champion inside her. Like the Gadarene swine, we plunge headlong towards the financial abyss. But few involved in the sport can imagine a life away from racing, and the nucleus and raison d'être of the whole business are the horses themselves.

This book traces the thoroughbred from the moment of conception through birth, the growing-up process, weaning, running out and eventually preparation for the sales. From the sale ring there follows long reining, breaking, gradual advanced discipline and finally preparation for the racecourse test. Along the way there are invariably setbacks and thwarted ambitions. But despite the inevitable disappointments there remains the gleaming hope, and occasional belief, that this could be the Good One. It is that shining dream that motivates the Racing World.

The Owner-Breeder

Bill Gredley

Bill Gredley is very much an owner and breeder of the new school. In the early nineteenth century the majority of racehorses were owned by the landed gentry, were bred on private estates and trained, for the main part, by private trainers. Training fees were around £10 per annum, and a useless or unsound horse would be shot – to the benefit of the breed. From time to time dispersal sales were held as a result of death or bankruptcy, allowing impetuous young men to buy into the best blood, but, in the main, racing – at least on New-market Heath – was the prerogative of the Jockey Club and the landed gentry.

A walk in the sun. The yearlings tone up for the sales with 40 minutes' exercise each morning from August onwards.

'My mother is called Interviewme, so I suppose the boss will give me a silly name…'
Eventually the Caerleon colt (bought in) was named Noelreac Julian.

Now the great names of the Victorian and Edwardian eras have faded away. In the 1890s, names like Derby, Durham, Ellesmere, Hardwicke, Montrose, Portland, Rosebery and Westminster dominated the sport. Now, all except Derby, and to a lesser extent Durham, are gone, either squeezed out by punitive death duties, or lost to the sport through male-line heirs with no interest.

Bill Gredley's Stetchworth Park was the home of Lord Ellesmere, whose famous stallion, Hampton, is buried on the estate. Lord Ellesmere's colours – red, white sleeves, black cap – are still carried by the few horses owned by his descendant, the Duke of Sutherland. Gredley bought Stetchworth House from the Duke in 1979. At the time the adjacent stud was owned by Colonel Douglas Gray, the former Director of the National Stud. When Gray retired in 1982, Gredley bought Stetchworth Park Stud.

Bill Gredley was born in London in 1933. He was not born with a silver spoon. He left school at the age of 16, and the following year began work as a clerk in a shipping office. It was in this City environment that he became streetwise and, after National Service with the Air Ministry, he moved back into City commerce. It was at this time that he became involved for the first time in property. The New Towns Commission had issued a compulsory purchase order on his grandmother's house in Essex and Gredley became actively

Polly Gredley is inconsolable. 'Her' filly Pretty Pollyanna *still* hasn't raced – and now she is
going to the sales!

Bill Gredley checks the foaling dates of the mares visiting Hadeer. On the left can be seen the tail of Hampton (Champion sire of 1887) who was buried on the stud.

involved in the fight against the steamrolling authority. Eventually, adequate compensation was paid to his grandmother and Gredley had learnt some important rules of the property world.

Now, 30 years later, from the launching pad of small speculations with borrowed cash in the early 1960s, he owns a group of companies with net assets in excess of £100 million. He deals mainly with City institutions and pension funds, and his success is based on ideas, integrity and an eye for a deal. Gredley, like most property men, loves 'a deal'. Gredley's gravitation towards the racing industry was motivated by youthful experiences and fond memories. 'I have always, since I was a kid, lived mainly in the country, and around horses. When I was first married, my wife and I set up home at Snaresbrook, near Wanstead. But in 1972 I bought a farm at Braughing in Hertfordshire, and, with the help of a manager, farmed 400 acres of arable land.

Back to our roots. The thoroughbred, a descendant over 300 years of the pure-bred Arab, enjoys nothing more than a roll in the sand.

'At the same time I was running my property business from offices in Charles Street, in Mayfair. I can't say that farming suited me. It was too slow. The manager was always wanting to show me that the wheat had grown an inch that week!'

With horses in mind, Gredley put some of the arable land to grass. Ponies were brought for his children, Jeremy and Sarah, who graduated to gymkhanas and hunter trials. It was in 1977 that Gredley's interest in racing caught fire. 'I spent an evening with the French trainer François Doumen while I was skiing in Gstaad. He reawakened my interest in horses. When I got back to England I happened to meet Clive and Maureen Brittain at a dinner party in a restaurant near Cambridge. I liked the idea of having a horse in training, but what I really wanted to do was to have some mares at Braughing.'

Clive Brittain remembers the meeting well. 'We hit it off straight away,' recalls Clive. 'We liked the same wines – and neither of us smoked! By the end of dinner Bill had decided to buy a dozen foals out of Group-placed mares. He was quick to anticipate the impact of the 'black-type' system in sales pedigrees. But the problem was that Braughing was going to take too long to put to grass. It was a farm. There was nowhere to put the foals!'

Gredley recalls: 'So I ended up buying two yearling fillies at the sales. One was called Purple Mark, who was trained by Clive; and the other Hot Lips Moll, trained by Bill Marshall. I'll always remember the first time Purple Mark ran. We went to Wolverhampton in a snowstorm. She started at 8–1 and won by a head in a driving finish. Clive was jumping about all over the place shouting, "We've won! We've won!" I turned to him and said, "I thought that was the point of the whole thing!"'

But despite his nonchalance at his extraordinary 'beginner's luck', Gredley was hooked. Now, 13 years later, Stetchworth Park Stud has 50 broodmares, 24 yearlings, and two stallions. The entire stock is valued in excess of £5 million. There are also over 30 horses in training.

Gredley's first good horse, Braughing, was bought the year of Purple Mark's pioneering success. His form was occasionally inconsistent, but as a four-year-old he won the Cambridgeshire, at Gredley's local course, at 50–1. It

Mare and foal enjoy creep-feeding as the summer sun scorches the grass.

was a famous moment. 'I was working hard at the time, and it was still really a running-in period for racing and I wasn't sure if I wanted to get involved. But Braughing clinched it.'

It was during this period that Gredley unhappily split up with his first wife, Pauline, sold the farm at Braughing and moved into Stetchworth House. Now his entire business interests, including property, bus companies, oil exploration, and other asset-based investments are controlled from Unex House, adjacent to his home on the stud. From his bedroom window he can look across the lush green paddocks of Stetchworth Park at clusters of year-lings grouped gregariously beneath age-old trees. 'I was very lucky to have the experience of Douglas Gray to guide me when I moved here. I was boarding my mares here while he still owned the stud, and he was a great help.'

Gredley has strong views on the financial structure of the industry and the way ahead. 'Everyone is forecasting gloom and doom in the racing and breed-ing industries at present, but I don't necessarily agree. It depends on which

'One doesn't wish to boast, but one is frightfully well connected...'

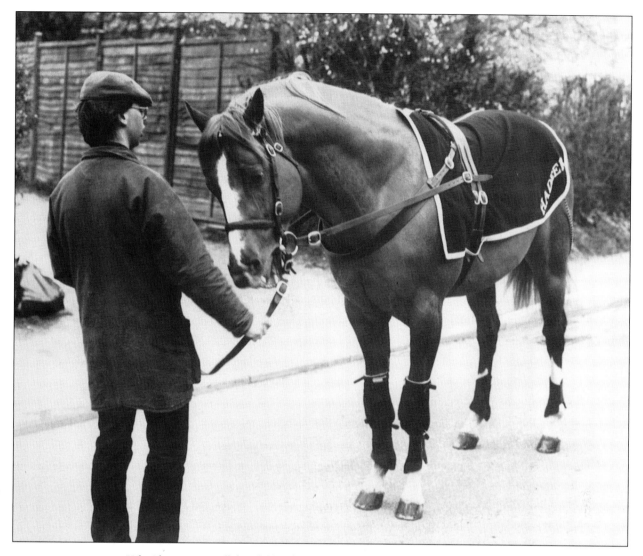

'Why I have to wear all this clobber for a simple walk...' Hadeer prepares for his daily 45-minute exercise.

side of the fence you are sitting. The Maktoum family are the strongest influence in racing at present, and their presence is to be welcomed. But the industry is far greater than any one influence. Fashions change ... people come and go ...

'As a commercial breeder, I see my future strategy as having a substantial number of good broodmares, accommodated on good paddocks, with good staff. But these commodities are costly to obtain, and maintain. If you splash out consistently on expensive stallion nominations, it becomes unworkable. Something has got to give.

'In my view, the correct area in which to rationalise is stallion fees. If you spend £100,000 on all of your stallion "covers", you'll end up in Carey Street. If, however, you spend between £10,000 and £40,000, and everything is well managed, then I believe that you still have a chance of making the business viable.

Pick of the bunch. The brown Secretariat colt, out of a Northern Dancer mare, is Stetchworth
Park's flagship at the forthcoming Tiffany Highflyer Sales.

'We are aiming to make a profit. The stud and racing activities are run
within the group as a section that has to be profitable, like every other section
of the business. Our objective is to breed a Champion for the market place.
Everything is for sale – and every yearling that we breed *goes* to the sales.'

Gredley's breeding strategy is a mixture of ancient and modern. 'As a rule, I
believe in the philosophy of breeding stout mares with fast stallions and vice
versa. But I make the occasional exception when the breeding consultants give
specific advice regarding a mating.'

Gredley's pride and joy at Stetchworth Park Stud is the stallion Hadeer. He
bought the handsome chestnut horse as a three-year-old from Sheik Maktoum
al Maktoum for just 13,000 guineas. Wearing Gredley's colours over the next
two seasons, Hadeer won three Group races, and was placed in the Sussex
Stakes, the Prix du Moulin and the Prix Jacques le Marois – three of the top
one-mile races in Europe. At the end of his racing career, Gredley syndicated
him at a valuation of £720,000. His first runners were competing in 1991.

On parade. A clutter of ankle-boots, to prevent cuts and grazes, litters the yearling yard.

Gredley pursues an aggressive policy with Hadeer. 'I believe you can *make* a stallion providing he has sufficient mares. I realise that it is an extreme and financially dangerous path to follow, but what I have done is to purpose-buy some exceptionally well-bred mares to be covered by Hadeer. This gives him the best possible chance of success. I don't think the commercial breeder has much choice other than to take such a chance. I can see a situation in the future whereby ten or so breeders would get together to *make* a particular stallion.'

Gredley also has a strictly-business approach to his horses in training. Last season almost every trainer in Britain increased his training fees by 20 per cent in the wake of the stable lads' pay increase and the community charge. Gredley refused to pay more than a 12 per cent increase. 'If a trainer can't afford to comply with my wishes then I will go to another trainer. Some of the increases

'Goodbye, old friend.' The grey colt by Cozzene spends his last night at the stud on the eve of the sales.

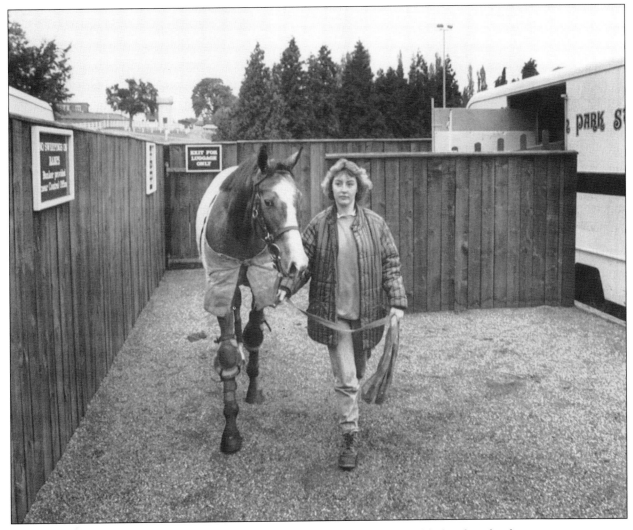

'Where are we now?' The Cozzene colt arrives at Tattersalls' Park Paddocks. Three days later
he was 'bought in' by the stud for 23,000 guineas and was named Environment Friend.

were unreasonable. Small owners did not have the inclination, or the courage,
to object. I feel bound to stick by my business principles.'

Gredley is now one of the top five British-based owners in terms of horses
in training. He is a prototype of the new breed of commercial owner-breeder.
In the past ten years the Maktoum family have acquired almost every top racehorse and broodmare that money and judgement could buy. Bill Gredley, for
one, is determined to take them on.

The Stud Groom

Michael Thomas

Michael Thomas, 41, does not conform to the traditional photo-fit of a stud groom. An appearance on *What's My Line* might inspire guesses like 'a telephone engineer' or 'a market trader'. But Thomas was born to the job and has spent all 25 years of his working life on thoroughbred studs. From leaving Newmarket Secondary School at the age of 17, he started work straightaway as

Kit inspection – stud-style. Michael Thomas wears the contemporary clothes of the young stud groom of the 1990s.

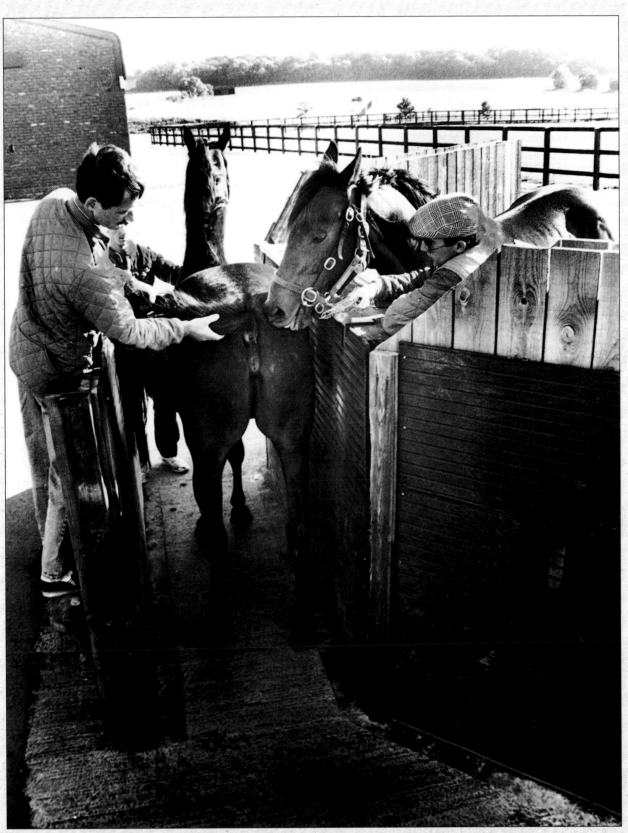

The 'teaser' at work. North Briton is allowed to look but not touch. The mare, if 'showing', will visit Hadeer in the covering barn.

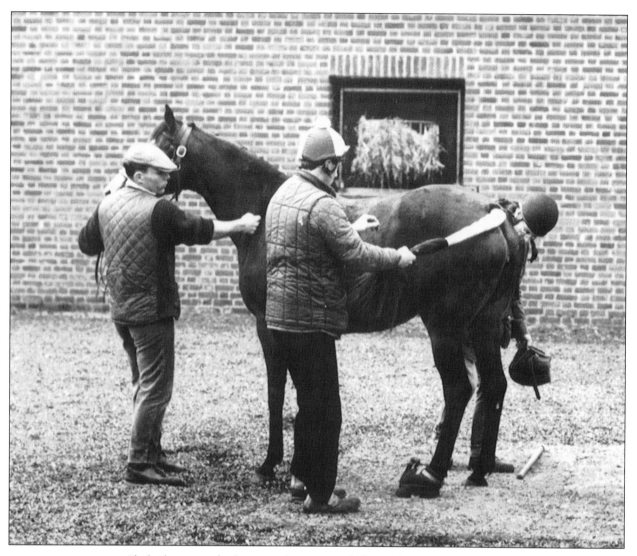

The bride prepares for the arranged marriage. Soft shoes reduce the risk of damage to the bridegroom.

a stud hand at Sir Kenneth Butt's Brook Stud, Cheveley, where his father was Yearling Man. Except for three months in Yorkshire in 1987, he has remained in or around Newmarket ever since.

'The great thing in those early days was that there was more time to learn the job – there were that many extra members of staff. The stud stood a stallion, Royal Record, who was restricted to 40 mares a season. In those days almost every stallion was. There were 15 or 16 mares on the stud and a staff of ten. My wage was about five pounds a week – and you earned 7s 6d (37½p) for "sitting-up"! Nowadays wages and conditions of work are vastly improved, both on studs and in racing stables, but fewer people either want to – or can afford to – come into the game. And those that do don't stay.'

For two seasons Thomas worked as stud groom at Stetchworth Park Stud. His day began at 6.30 a.m. He would walk round the yard, and during the summer the paddocks, to assess the behaviour patterns of mares and

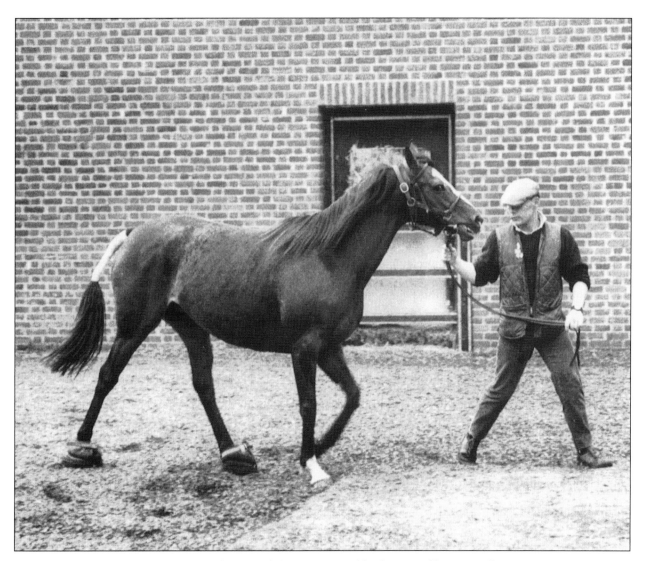

Prepared and 'ready', the mare is led in. 'Come on, old girl – grin and bear it.' 'Well *you* try
walking in these silly shoes!'

check their wellbeing. 'You can learn a great deal just standing and watching
mares,' he says. 'Very often they will "show" to each other as much as to the
"teaser".' The 'teaser' at Stetchworth Park Stud is North Briton, an exceptionally well-bred horse of less than average ability during an undistinguished racing career. His role is to determine through restrained physical contact at the
teasing board whether or not a mare is ready to be covered. As a reward for his
frustrating duties, the 'teaser' is 'given' two or three mares a season. In 1986,
when a rather skittish mare called Branitska was threatening to kick the stallion Hadeer to kingdom come, North Briton was invited to enjoy the dubious
pleasure of mounting her instead. The result of this union was a colt called Call
To Arms, one of the outstanding two-year-olds of 1989!

During the spring – the covering season lasts from February to July – the
stud hands arrive at 7.30 a.m.; the yearlings and 'heavy' mares are led out to
the paddocks; and 'teasing' (or 'trying') begins with the barren and maiden

The business of doing pleasure. Hadeer earns the stud a further £3000 – subject to
'live' ammunition.

mares, and mares that have foaled early. A mare that shows herself to be in the
correct sexual condition will be covered at 9.30. Most stallions have two
covering periods a day. The 4.30 cover is normally reserved for mares that
'walk in' from nearby studs when they are assessed by their stud grooms to be
'ready'.

'We liked to get Hadeer to the barn about ten minutes before covering so
that he knew exactly what was happening,' Thomas says. 'Quite a number of
mares "walk in" around Newmarket: there are so many local studs. The
trouble is, people ring up and expect an immediate service. It's not quite as
easy as that! Hadeer seems a very brave horse. Some mares have to be covered
very close to ovulation, and can be very ticklish. He is not bothered. The more
they move the better he likes it!'

At 8.30 a.m. the vet arrives to examine mares, take swabs and deal with
day-to-day problems. The stud's official vet is Nick Wingfield-Digby (see

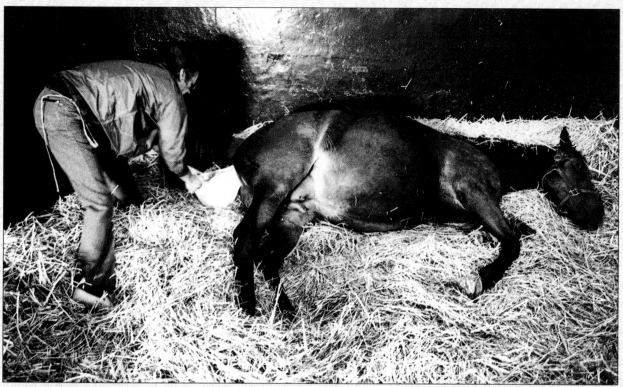

The joy of birth. Michael Thomas assists a smooth foaling. The front feet and head are first to emerge, inside the foetal membrane.

The stud groom removes the foal from the foetal membrane, but the umbilical cord (out of view) remains intact until the mare eventually gets to her feet.

page 39), but on routine days his assistant Sarah Stoneham stands in. Meanwhile, Hadeer enjoys 45 minutes of exercise on a carefully selected route around the stud. Nowadays, a stallion will cover anything from 40 up to 70 mares a year. The horse is syndicated in 40 shares on his retirement from racing, and each shareholder has one breeding right per season. However, several studs, notably in Ireland, sell up to a further 30 nominations to the stallion with proceeds divided between the stud and the 40 shareholders.

Stetchworth Park Stud has over 50 resident mares, several of whom will be covered by Hadeer. So invariably there will be foals and yearlings by Hadeer on the stud to advertise their father. Mares choose to have their foals at nightfall or during the night. Some Arab tribes have strong superstitions regarding foals born during daylight and destroy them immediately. 'Sitting-up' with foaling mares is a duty undertaken by staff in rotation. When a mare shows signs of foaling the 'sitter-up' immediately alerts the stud groom, who takes charge. Only if complications arise is the vet summoned. But most foalings go smoothly and are completed within 15 minutes.

Half an hour after birth: the mare admires the result of 11 months' hard work.

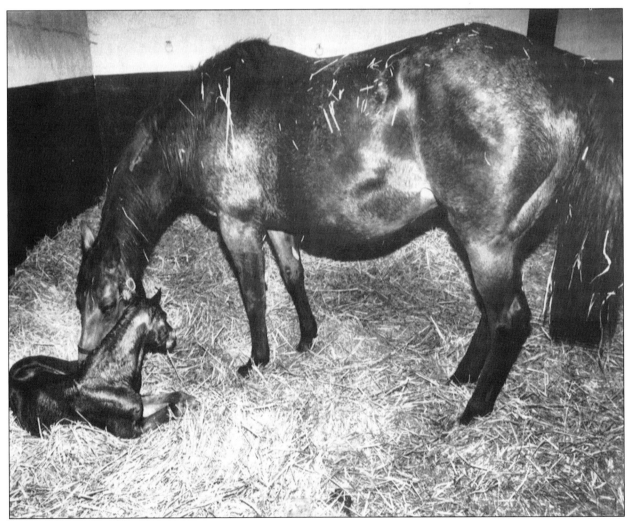

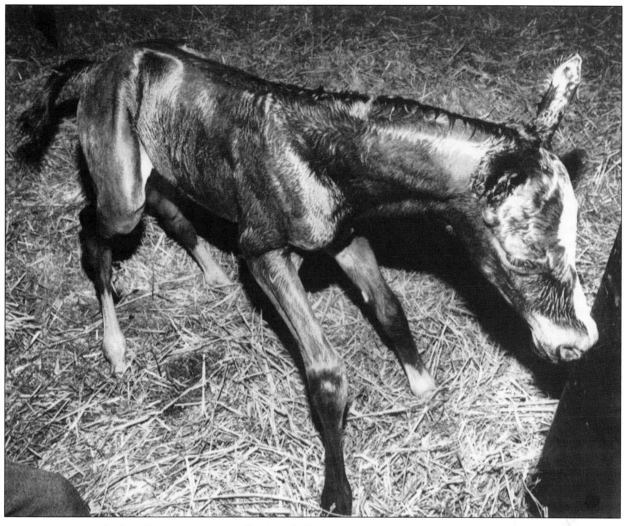

The first faltering steps. It normally takes a foal between 30 and 90 minutes to struggle to its feet.

The stud groom – and Bill Gredley – will invariably be keeping an eye on an expected foaler by means of television monitors in their respective houses. The main yard at Stetchworth Park has two foaling boxes and two adjacent boxes for the next wave of foaling mares. The stud groom will check with the sitter-up at 8 p.m. as to what degree the foalers are waxed up and showing signs that 'tonight's the night'. Mares can remain 'imminent' for up to 12 days. At £35 per night, this can make 'sitting-up' an expensive luxury for the owner of the mare! Michael Thomas will go to bed at 9.30 p.m. and expect to be awoken somewhere between midnight and 3 a.m.

'Over the years I've been lucky with foaling mares,' says Thomas. 'The worst foaling I ever had was, needless to say, with a valuable mare. The mare got so far and then stopped. Eventually we dragged the foal out, but it was short of oxygen, and the off-hind stifle and hock were all fused; it would never have stood up. We had no alternative but to put it down. By and large, if within 20 minutes of the breaking of the waters the foal is not on the ground we've got problems, and we call the vet.

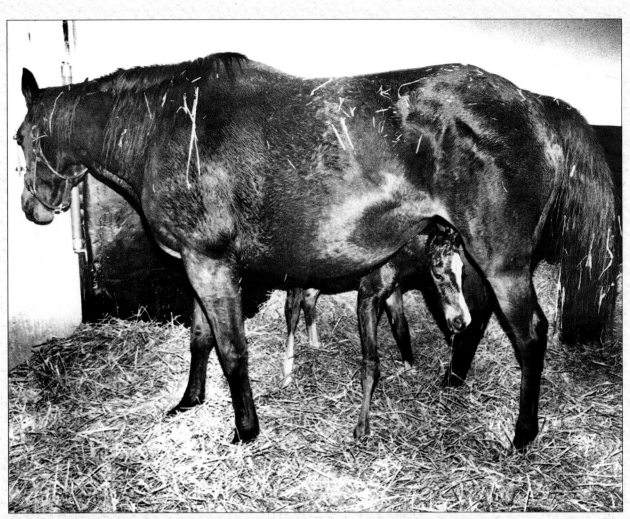

'Now, where's the milk bar?' The new-born foal searches unhesitatingly for the mare's udder.

'Every foaling is different and, whatever the hour, you never feel tired when the adrenalin is running. There is nothing more satisfying than seeing a fine, healthy foal.' A healthy foal will struggle to its feet within 30 to 90 minutes of its birth and go straight to its mother's udder. After a couple of days, the mare and foal will be turned out into the indoor barn, or, if the weather is especially clement, into a small outdoor paddock. If the mare has enjoyed a smooth and comfortable foaling, and has avoided any subsequent infection of the uterus, she can be 'tried' on the foal heat (about seven days after foaling) – and the entire 11-month cycle begins again.

Foals remain with their mothers for five months, when the time comes for the newborn to be weaned. This is a sad and traumatic process which involves confining the foal to a box for four or five days, while the mare is moved to as distant a paddock as possible, out of earshot. Thereafter the weaned foals of each sex are reunited in a fresh paddock, and enter the phase akin to a child going to boarding school. Some foals are sent to be sold at Newmarket's December Sales, while the majority spend the next 12 months with one major 'examination' in mind – the yearling sales.

A step into the world outside. This is the correct way to hold a young foal. To do otherwise exerts too much pressure on the foal's chest. The foal wears a head-collar from day one.

For a commercial stud the yearling sales at Doncaster in September, and Newmarket and Kill in Co. Kildare in October, constitute the most important four weeks of the year. The stud is largely financed by revenue from the sale of their yearlings. Mares and foals are also sold at the December Sales, but yearlings are the 'dream' market. In the mid-1980s, with the influx of Arab buyers, yearling prices exceeded £1 million on several occasions. Now that Arabs are less disposed to bid against one another, the market has levelled out to a rational plane. But the dream remains to produce at least a half-million pound yearling.

After three days mare and foal venture out into a small restricted paddock. For the first week
the foal sticks close to its mother, suckling and studying behaviour patterns.

With such colossal rewards available, the business of preparing yearlings has become mega-professional. The process begins from the time the foals are weaned, and form their own private clubs and cliques out in the paddock. The competitive herd instinct creates a major risk of epiphysitis at this stage. This is an inflammation of the growth plates at the bottom end of the cannon bone, above the fetlock joint. It is caused by foals putting undue pressure on immature and underdeveloped bones. If the foal has poor conformation and uneven weight distribution the risk is heightened. Incorrect diet; lack of calcium; and vitamin deficiency are the other causes. The end product is a period of lameness and, in some cases, a malformation of the joint which remains with the horse throughout his life. Epiphysitis can also affect yearlings at the top end of the cannon bone, causing a bony growth on the inside of the knee. 'It's usually caused by foals galloping on joints that are re-shaping,' says Thomas. 'Foals grow a lot between six and 12 months and they go through a difficult phase.'

The foals, who become yearlings on 1 January, are brought in at night during the winter and spring. Most studs leave the yearlings out from Guineas week onwards, but Bill Gredley prefers to keep them in at night until the assessor from Tattersalls sales visits the stud in mid-May. This is a vital visit. Upon his assessment hinges the decision as to whether the yearling is sold at the prestigious Highflyer Sales – where prices can exceed £500,000 – or the more cosmopolitan October Open Sale, where bargains are often to be found. 'If they're out all the time they are more liable to pick up lumps, bumps and cuts, which are unsightly and *could* influence an assessor,' says Thomas.

The yearling colts spend much of the spring and summer in the 18-acre park behind Stetchworth House. It is perfect, verdant stud land, selected with pride by the Duke of Sutherland 150 years ago. 'It's always safer to keep colts in large numbers rather than small groups,' believes Thomas. 'There is less fighting – and they always settle well in the park. Personally I like to bring them in twice a week during the summer. It makes life easier for the blacksmith; it makes them easier to handle; and it makes them "box sane". Otherwise, when they do come in they are liable to climb the wall of the box.'

The yearlings begin their preparation for the sales during the second week of August. They are walked in hand for 40 minutes per day as part-education and part-toning-up process. Nowadays, an attractive yearling needs to be exceptionally fit at the sales. An increasing number of 'spotters', agents, trainers and owners ensure that an attractive, well-bred yearling will be pulled out of his box and walked to and fro up to 60 times a day. The procedure is exhausting for a yearling – let alone a foal. A yearling will have worn a headcollar from the first week of his life, but the period of sales preparation will be the first occasion he has worn a bridle.

'Depending on how quickly they mouth to the bit, we like to lunge them as soon as possible in the indoor school,' says Thomas. 'Nowadays, they are wind-tested within 30 days of the sales, so they must be fit for that. Some of them find it difficult to coincide their breath with their action. We also use a horse-walker when they're walking in hand well enough. The yearlings going

Foals stay with mares for up to five or six months. Then they are weaned and join the other members of their sex in a foals' paddock.

to the October Open always do this for the last two weeks. The yearlings are fed three times a day during preparation for the sales. But we don't *change* their diet,' says Thomas.

And so the great day comes when the yearlings are boxed for their first journey away from the stud – the three-mile trip to Park Paddocks, New-market, home of the yearling sales. The next three days are the busiest period of their young lives.

The Vet

Nick Wingfield-Digby

Nick Wingfield-Digby is widely regarded as the best veterinary surgeon in Newmarket. He is certainly one of the busiest. His workload is extensive and the pressure on him intense. He is responsible for veterinary work at four racing stables and no fewer than eight studs.

His day begins with a visit to the offices of his practice, Rossdale & Hunt, at 8 a.m. From there he travels a mile to his first port of call, the Marquess of Har-

Nick Wingfield-Digby performs a uterine biopsy to discover the cause of infertility in a barren mare. Obligatory clothing consists of waterproof overalls and sterile plastic sleeves. For safety's sake the mare is confined in a metal stock.

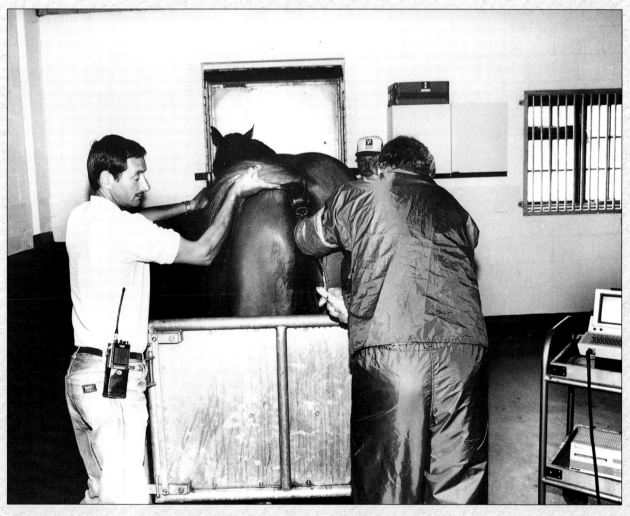

The vet examines the biopsy at the practice's headquarters. The aim of his research is to ensure that the mare conceives successfully the following year.

tington's Side Hill Stud, on the outskirts of Newmarket. His duties include examining new arrivals and routine gynaecological work like swabbing and scanning mares for possible pregnancy. He travels with a mobile scanner in the back of the car. There follow discussions with the stud manager and stud groom. He then moves on to his next stud, Northmore, a 350-acre private stud owned by Hugh van Cutsem. By 10.30 a.m. he will have arrived at Stetchworth Park Stud, where his responsibilities cover the main stud and the satellite studs at nearby Dullingham Ley. Between 11.30 and 12 he visits the nearby Collin Stud, whereafter he returns home for lunch.

After lunch he embarks upon what he calls his 'Bury [St. Edmunds] Run', embracing the West Stow, Langham Hall and Campbell Studs. Then it's back to Newmarket for evening stables where the horses trained by Harry Thomson Jones come under his direct responsibility. He oversees three other stables, but there his duties are delegated, except in major crises. After stables, he dictates reports onto tapes for audio-typists; clears up other paperwork; and collects non-urgent messages from other casual clients. On a good day, he will just be home in time to read a bedtime story to his young son.

Nick's box of tricks. The vet's travelling surgery includes antibiotics, ointments, anti-inflammatory drugs, surgery kit, blood, a syringe and sampling tubes. Assistant Jenny Küchel wields a tooth rasp.

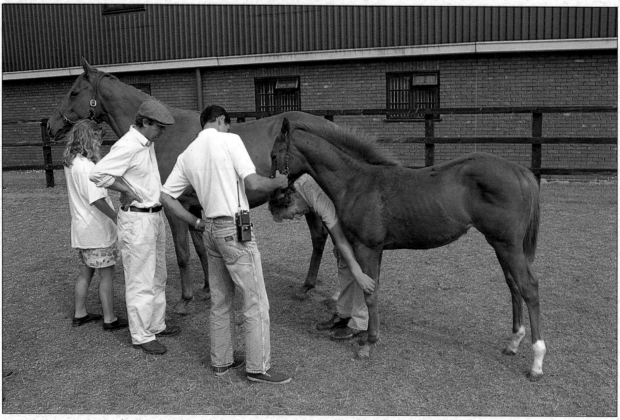

Stud groom Nigel Wright looks on as the vet examines a foal for epiphysitis – inflammation of the growth plates. Almost certainly the vet will recommend a different programme of diet and exercise.

And then comes the emergency call … 'During the stud season [January to July] it is effectively a seven-day week,' he sighs. 'I work until lunchtime on Saturday, and until 10.30 on Sunday morning.' What is sacrosanct is his cricket. He plays for the Suffolk Gentlemen, the Newmarket Trainers XI and occasionally the MCC, bowling right-arm medium pace with notable length and accuracy.

During his working day he may encounter: stallions with libido or vene-real problems; mares that are diseased, infertile, have aborted, are bad moth-ers, or are dangerously mad; foals that are 'wobblers', 'barkers' (suffering from convulsions), have colic, hepatitis, nephritis, and a great many other -itis con-ditions; horses in training that are neurotic, lame, or simply off-colour, in other words have a 'virus'. At any one time Wingfield-Digby will be respon-sible for upwards of 750 horses. His practice collectively looks after 35 stables and 30 studs, and the partners will often consult one another. 'I suppose the basis of our skills is the early detection of problems that an unskilled man would take longer to isolate. To achieve that requires intimate knowledge of the horses, and a good relationship with the people who enable you to see what is wrong. The keynote is accurate diagnosis and correct immediate re-medial action. Where possible I try to suggest alternatives in *management* rather than prescription of drugs.

'On the stud side, the first target is to be satisfied with normal behaviour patterns in new-born foals and to attempt to avert the problems that can knock a foal for six. To begin with it is just a case of taking routine blood tests and carrying out regular physical examinations, then simply monitoring growth and freedom from development problems.' The first hours and days of a foal's life are vitally important as the foal is acutely receptive to its environment and to procedures.

'As for mares,' he says, 'my job is to get them in foal as quickly and efficiently as possible, expending the minimum of management time. Nowadays, the vet is the linch-pin of the reproduction side of public studs. He is involved in every stage, including assessing the correct time to cover mares. Previously this was the exclusive province of the stud groom.'

Nick Wingfield-Digby, with his weather-worn husky and crumpled corduroy trousers, looks every inch a vet in the Herriot mould. But his background is unusual. His father, the Venerable Basil Wingfield-Digby, was Archdeacon of Sarum in Wiltshire. A sporting vicar, he rowed for Christchurch, Oxford, and enjoyed shooting, fishing and diocesan cricket. Nick's younger brother, the Reverend Andrew Wingfield-Digby, was captain of Dorset CC and is managing director of Christians in Sport. In 1990 he was appointed chaplain to the British team at the Commonwealth Games.

'If it's mid-morning it must be Northmore…' The vet carries out a routine assessment of a foal's conformation and growth at Hugh van Cutsem's Northmore Stud.

The lungeing ring. A yearling filly is lunged to check for any possible respiratory problem. A wind report should accompany every yearling to the sales.

Nick had a clear vision of his life before leaving Sherborne School. He went straight to Bristol University, and embarked on a five-year course of veterinary science. At the end of this he was encouraged by two distinguished practitioners to continue with post-graduate education and was awarded a scholarship by the Horserace Betting Levy Board. He spent a further year studying mares that were difficult to get in foal, whilst doing practical work at the Sandley

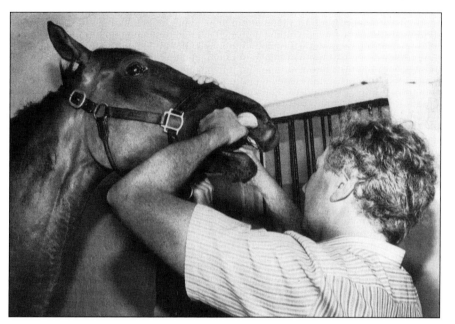

All in a day's work. The vet grasps a two-year-old's tongue in his left hand to avoid being bitten as he examines the colt's milk teeth.

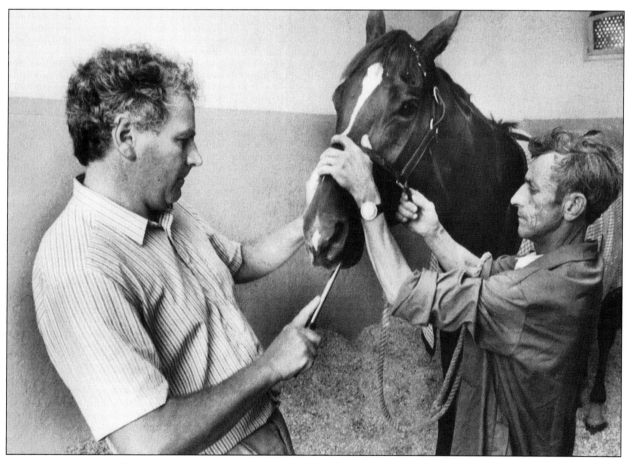

'This won't hurt a bit...' Every young horse needs routine rasping of the molar teeth to prevent sharp edges from causing sore gums.

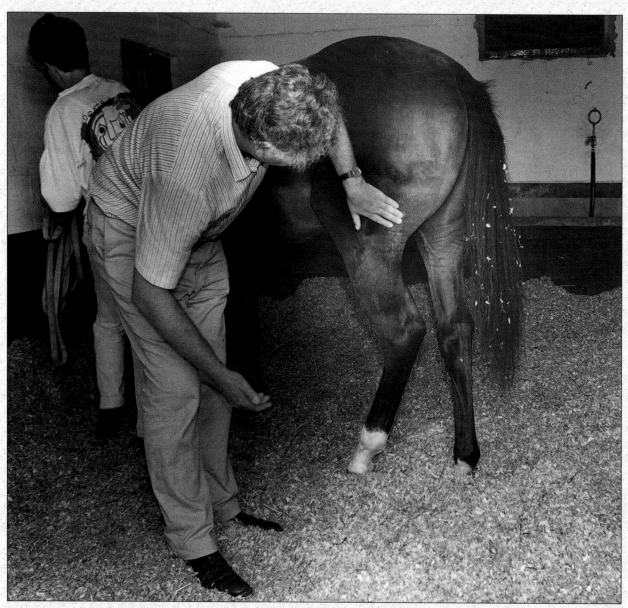

This yearling's haematoma (blood blister) resulted from a muscle injury. The blister was lanced to release the fluid. At the sales, the Ajdal colt (foaled 18 June) made 46,000 guineas.

Stud at Gillingham, Dorset. By now he was irrevocably drawn to the reproductive side of the thoroughbred world. A valuable period of practical work with the equine foetus at Bristol University's Department of Surgery was followed by an invitation to work as house surgeon during the long vacation. It was in November 1973 that he moved to Newmarket to join the practice of Peter Rossdale.

'Actually, for the first two years I was employed to build up the dog and cat side of the business,' he admits wryly. 'But horses were my overwhelming interest. Newmarket had *everything*. It was the perfect place to practise – and I couldn't wait to get involved.' Peter Rossdale had other ideas. 'How would you like to go to Iran?' he said one morning.

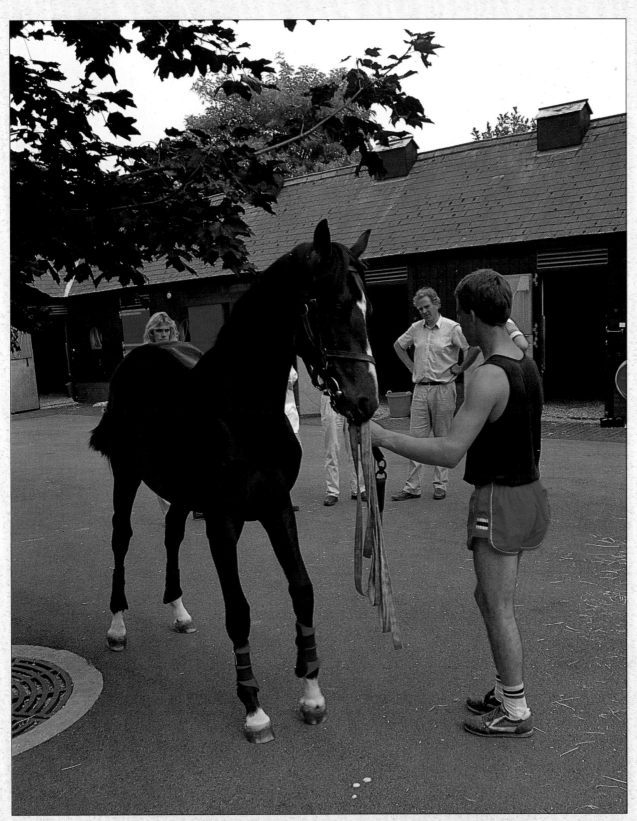

'I'm not sure about him…' The vet appraises a colt. His notes: '… epiphysitis … off-set at the knee…' A prospective buyer would add: 'weak; straight in front; light of bone'. Not surprisingly the colt failed to reach his reserve at the October Open Sales.

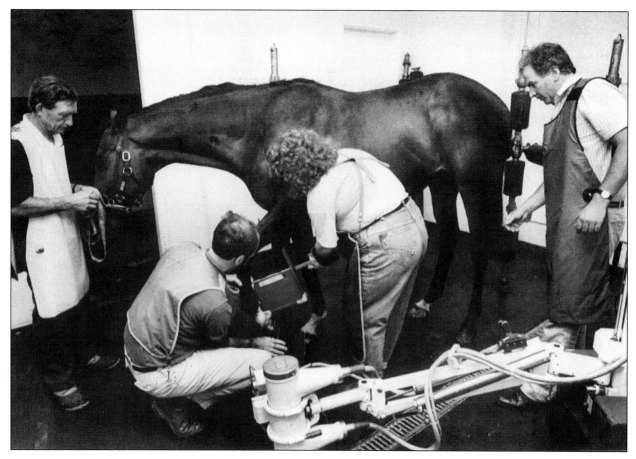

A two-year-old submits to radiography with modern powerful x-ray equipment. The suspected damage is to a sesamoid bone at the back of the fetlock joint.

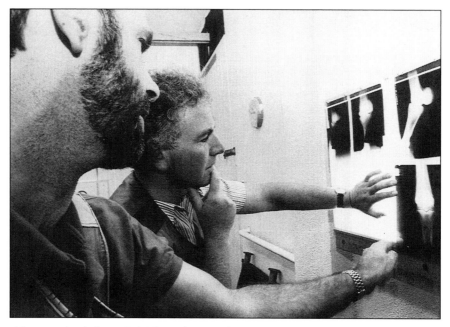

The vet and radiologist, Rob Pilsworth, assess the x-rays on a viewing screen. Close scrutiny reveals a hairline fracture to the sesamoid. The prescribed treatment: six months' rest.

Nurse, anaesthetist and surgeon help position a horse for surgery to the respiratory tract. The second nurse (left) holds a fibre-optic endoscope in her left hand, and the control-panel for the operating table in her right. The padded table lifts on a hydraulic ramp. After surgery it lowers onto running rails and slides through the doors (right) into a padded recovery room.

The brief was to work as veterinary surgeon to the Imperial Stables in Tehran. The Shah was building a racetrack with a view to importing racehorses from Australia, South Africa and Europe. There would also be creole racing with Arab and Turkoman horses. There was massive Western investment in Iran, while the racetrack was to be financed by Hong Kong interests. 'It was a terrific experience,' Nick recalls. 'There were grand military parades – of course with a vet always on duty. The Shah was totally omnipotent. I suppose I was working for one of the most exclusive clientèles in the world – just the Shah and his personal friends. Now they are virtually all dead.'

With the storm clouds of revolution gathering, Nick accepted an invitation from the Australian vet Percy Sykes to travel to Sydney for two months of the racing season. 'I did routine work for two great trainers in Tommy Smith and Bart Cummings but, more important, I had packed a uterine biopsy forcep and flew round New South Wales examining mares that had failed to get

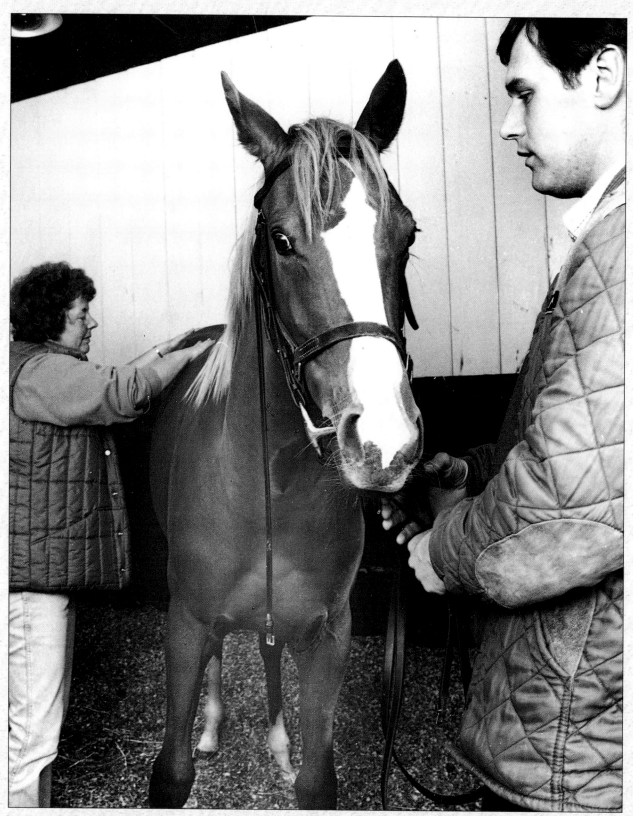

Alternative treatment. Carol Whitworth is one of a growing group of independent physiotherapists who practise back manipulation. Here she probes – successfully, it appears – for an area of discomfort.

in foal.' By now Nick was yearning to return home and, travelling across America via veterinary schools in San Francisco, New York, and Lexington, Kentucky, he finally touched down back in Newmarket. 'It was great experience working abroad, but Newmarket is the best place to be. There is no other place where everything is in such numbers and of such quality – and it's all nearby.'

Now it is Nick's duty to ensure that up to 90 per cent of mares at Stetchworth Park Stud are successfully in foal – and breed healthy foals. 'There is no doubt the performance of individual mares has improved greatly thanks to veterinary progress,' he states. 'There is less venereal disease nowadays and since the incidence of CEM [Contagious Equine Metritis] in the late 1970s, stud hygiene has improved out of all knowledge.' But the irony remains that despite giant strides forward in veterinary science, thoroughbred breeding remains the most inexact of all sciences. Ask Bill Gredley – and Call To Arms!

The Bloodstock Agent

John Warren

John Warren is one of the bright young men of the racing scene. He has made a name as a shrewd and successful buyer of thoroughbred yearlings. From spending a few thousand pounds on cheap horses for a handful of friends, he can now bid up to six figures for owners like multi-millionaire Dr Michael Smurfit and for several up-market syndicates. But the foundations of success are fragile. He knows that two or three expensive flops could undermine his reputation. Furthermore, like a football manager, his reputation depends upon the achievements of others. Once a horse that he has bought moves on to the selected trainer, he can only watch anxiously from the periphery.

'Nice after-shave...' John Warren chats with a friend at the Marquess of Hartington's Side Hill Stud.

The back-up team. Lady CarolynWarren and her brother Lord Harry Herbert inspect a potential purchase. Lord Harry is Racing Executive of Kennet Valley Thoroughbreds.

The battlegrounds of Warren's professional life are the sale rings at Keeneland (Kentucky), Newmarket, Kill and Fairyhouse. The sale season lasts from Keeneland in July until Newmarket in October. During that time Warren and his competitors will assess and evaluate up to 7000 yearlings and view in person between 1500 and 2000. At the end of a gruelling six-week marathon in September and October he will have bought between 40 and 50 horses. The sternest challenge and biggest ball-game is the Keeneland July Sale where, in temperatures of up to 90 degrees, the Maktoum family from Dubai have been known to bid beyond $10 million for the apple of their eye. Warren's arena is the upper–middle market.

'The problem with dealing at the top end is that there are too many wealthy people. If they really want a horse they are almost bound to succeed. In that rarefied climate it's easy to get carried away. I feel confident up to the $100,000 price range. There are plenty of Group race winners to be bought up to that price. The advantage of buying colts at that level is that there are so many markets to sell on to after they have raced in Britain.'

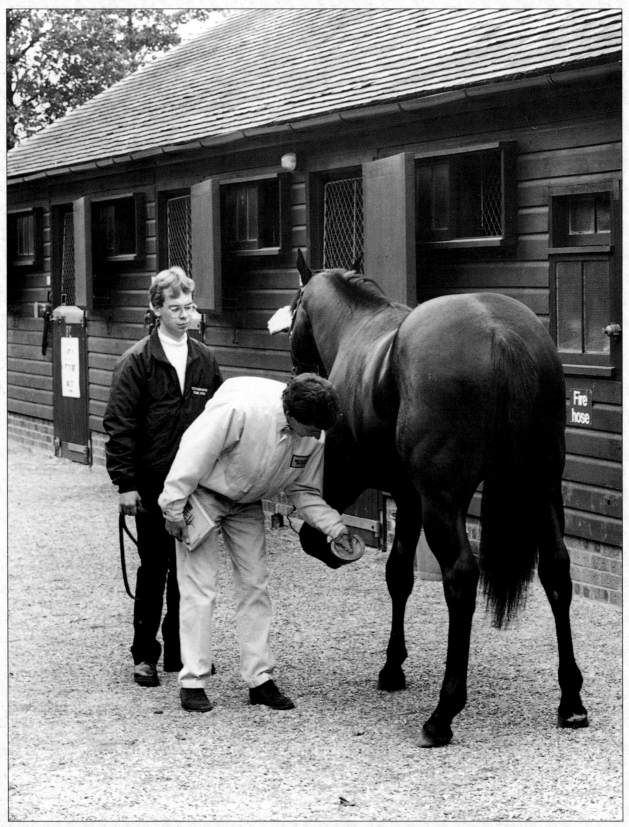

'No foot, no horse.' Warren is an expert on horses' feet – an area to which American buyers pay close attention.

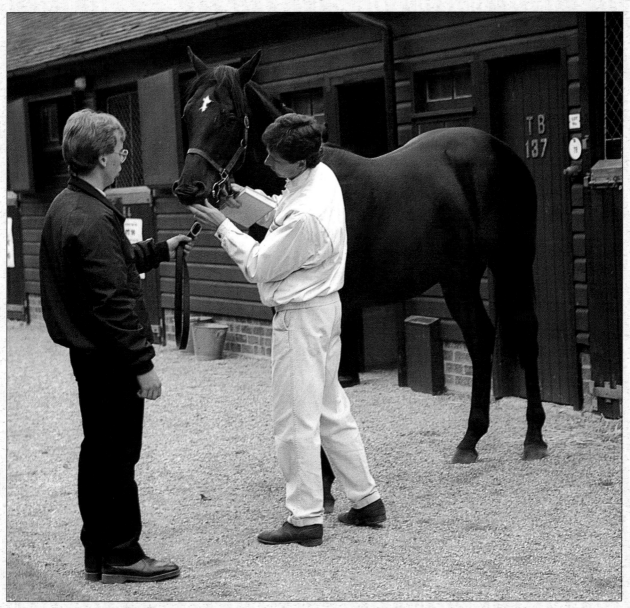

Warren checks the Chief Singer yearling for a possible parrot-mouth (malformation of the lower jaw), a condition which creates difficulty in digesting food.

Warren will rarely buy more than three or four horses at Keeneland. The market is invariably strong and value is elusive. It is an arena where an international agent must be seen to be in evidence and where useful contacts are made. But the strength of black gold and the mighty dollar is almost impossible to overcome. So the Tattersalls Tiffany Highflyer and the Goffs Million are the markets where Warren expects to conduct his most significant business. The brilliant concept of a million-pound horserace restricted to graduates of one select sale was the brainchild of Goffs' former supremo, Jonathan Irwin. Through his imaginative vision the 'Cartier Million' was born – and the Tattersalls Tiffany Highflyer Stakes quickly followed on. In the case of Goffs, just 250 horses sold at the Million Sale were qualified to race 12 months later for the first prize of IR£500,000. Tattersalls select the top 300 sales entries who, in 1990 and 1991, qualified for a £500,000 prize each for colts and fillies. It was with a view to winning the inaugural Goffs Million that the up-market Kennet Valley syndicate was created by Lord Harry Herbert in 1987. John Warren bought four yearlings for the syndicate. The second and third placings achieved by Miss Demure and French Pretender netted the syndicate IR£300,000.

Up to 30 years ago it was racehorse trainers who would bid for and buy the majority of yearlings at sales. Many from the old school would simply stand by the side of the ring and bid when a certain yearling caught his eye. Nowadays, with thoroughbreds capable of attaining ultimately a value of up to £20 million, the process is infinitely more elaborate. 'When I first started buying yearlings I would begin by looking at them on the studs during summer, but I don't do that now. I found that by sales time they had changed so much, and often gone backwards, that it was counter-productive. Also, if there was something that I didn't like at the time, I found it difficult to eliminate from my mind. When I next saw the horse, I was blinded by preconceived ideas. The only advantage, I found, was being able to assess a horse's temperament.

'So now the start of the cycle is the arrival of the sales catalogue. Firstly, I will get someone to "mark up" my catalogue – that's to say, denote the ratings of the yearlings' dams and previous produce of the mare. Added to that will be comments about the family's going-preference, preferred distances and the trainers of the produce so far. Armed with that information, I will eliminate the lots of no interest on pedigree. The first yearlings arrive at the sales several days in advance. If physically possible, I like to look at every lot in the sale that I haven't eliminated. At the Highflyer Sale, I will probably look at *all* of the horses. At Goffs, I strike out 30 per cent on pedigree or foaling date. I would not, for instance, buy a May foal to win the "Million". In the case of Keeneland, I try to arrive between seven and ten days before the sale; one has to drive *miles* around Keeneland to see all the horses … there are five here, six there, and so on. They will have come from all over the place to be prepared for the sale.

'At Newmarket, having looked at the first day lots, we have a further elimination process, and finally draw up a list of horses to be examined by the vet. When that has been done, I will get together with the vet, and take in his advice. Back home, I will do more pedigree research – especially with fillies. For instance, whom has the mare visited in the past two years, and who has trained the previous foals? On the morning of the sale I will have a final view of the short-listed horses following the vet's comments. I don't like to visit a horse too often – there is a limit to how much you want to show your hand. If the yearling is up to scratch on the third inspection, we will work out a valuation. This is an inexact science. There are so many changing circumstances up till the last second.

'There are only a handful of horses in the sale that you are *desperate* to buy; and it is only really in the pre-parade ring that you can assess their value accurately. You will pick up strong vibes if men like James Delahooke [the agent] and Guy Harwood are lingering. Then you must ask yourself – shall I up the

Horses, horses, everywhere… Warren studies a yearling catalogue as the lengthy international sales season approaches.

The agent assesses the Secretariat colt. 'I like him. I was only critical because on the whole people prefer Secretariat *fillies*.'

ante? I paid far too much, for instance, for a colt by Auction Ring at the Cartier Million Sale in 1989. We had short-listed five and missed the other four. We *had* to have a horse for the "Million", and he was the best of the lot. I knew we would have to spend money – the vendor was Alan Lillingston, the best sales-man in the business. We found we were bidding against Henry Cecil. I bid IR200,000 guineas and everyone thought I was mad. There was only one thing we could do – we sent him to Henry to train!

'I bought 42 yearlings that autumn. Luckily trainers seem to like what I buy. I buy "two-year-old types" – ie, horses that are ready to go on with, as

John and Carolyn Warren appraise a recent purchase for Kennet Valley Thoroughbreds who is boarding during education at father-in-law, Lord Carnarvon's Highclere Stud.

opposed to big, backward, leggy "three-year-old types". I like to keep in touch with my clients' trainers on a week-to-week basis. Trainers are always liable to criticise if they haven't been involved in the buying! We decide which horses to send to which trainers six weeks after the Highflyer Sales. Obviously we have our own view about which trainer suits what type of horse. In the interim the horses will have been to a "spelling farm" [so called because horses visit for a spell or period] – usually Highclere Stud where there is so much land and a very good "breaking" team. Trainers are generally happy with the way our horses have been broken. But there is always one horse who will let you down! By February there are usually strong vibes about a horse. If it's a *bad* vibe then almost without exception you can fear the worst! An above-average horse will usually be showing his trainer *something* by February.

'I rarely buy more than five or six horses at any sale. I cannot rationally buy more, whilst keeping an eye on "value". In 1989 we decided to have a fillies syndicate for the Tattersalls Tiffany race. There were 250 colts in the sale and only 150 fillies – but the two races were worth £500,000 each. It seemed to make sense, but it didn't work. There was no value in the sale. The Maktoums were buying and our valuations went out of the window.

'I am difficult to work with at the sales. If clients give me hassle I will often tell them to go off and buy for themselves. After all, they have only seen one horse, and not the rest – so they have no relative judgement. I always remember Dick Hern saying to me once: "Do you have that horse in your *mind's eye*?" At the sales, I do have. I have a photographic memory for a horse. I can remember every small detail. Once a horse has made an impression on me, it is indelible. Later, I will return to view the horse as a *character*, as opposed to a specimen.

'It is very helpful at the sales to see the good, old-fashioned stud grooms year after year. You can trust them implicitly. They know that if they pull the wool over your eyes, you won't come back the following year. And the same applies to stud managers. For instance, Chris Harper of Whitsbury Stud is marvellous. If I ask him if a horse is all right, I know he'll tell me the truth. Of course, buying yearlings has to be a team effort. My brother-in-law [Lord Harry Herbert] is especially valuable during the pre-looking stage. My wife, Carolyn, is a very good natural judge, and can talk sensibly when the clients pitch up. Furthermore, she is extremely helpful at reminding me of things like the vet's list. She always has something to contribute.'

And so it was that John Warren came to view the consignment from Stetchworth Park Stud at the 1989 Tiffany Highflyer Sale. 'There were two that caught my attention. Firstly, the Chief Singer colt [ex Hi Tech Girl]. He was an unusual type for a Chief Singer – very wide beamed. And the Secretariat colt. I liked him. I was only critical because on the whole people prefer Secretariat fillies. I remember two years earlier at Keeneland there was a very good-looking dark brown horse – like him – that was sold for a fortune of money. He was no good at all. So in the end, his sex and his colour put me off ...' Ian Balding saw the Secretariat colt – Secret Silence – and nothing put *him* off. He bought him for 130,000 guineas.

The Auctioneer

Richard Mildmay-White

Richard Mildmay-White is next in line to be senior partner at Tattersalls Ltd. Tattersalls are the largest and most celebrated horse auctioneers in the British Isles, with an annual turnover of £100 million. Tattersalls' most important sales are during October and December, but the involvement exists from 1 January onwards. Tattersalls is an unquoted limited company, the bulk of

After inspection in the Upper Sales Paddock, a yearling enters the ring to await the auctioneer's sales pitch.

Grooming kit. The paraphernalia of preparing a yearling to look his best.

A case of stage-fright? The Secretariat colt casts an anxious eye at the assembly of potential buyers.

whose shares are owned by the four senior directors, Michael Watt, Capt. Kenneth Watt, Bruce Deane and Mildmay-White. With property and goodwill that are the envy of their competitors, they are subject to constant takeover enquiries, but no director is disposed to sell.

'Happily, we are not vulnerable to takeover,' says Mildmay-White with a hint of pride.

The Tattersalls year begins with a series of policy meetings. 'For most of January we argue about what we are going to do in the coming year,' smiles Mildmay-White. As early as February letters are sent out to breeders and regular vendors inviting entries for the prestige yearling sales – the Highflyer and October Open – which take place during the first and third weeks of October. Replies are requested by early March. The Highflyer is the jewel in the Tattersalls crown. It is restricted to 300 yearlings – the cream. It is a remarkable barometer of the health of the industry that demand for Highflyer places far exceeds availability.

'What am I bid…?' This is the moment towards which the past 18 months have been directed.
All will be over in less than three minutes.

When the entry forms are finally received, a panel of three pedigree experts sit down to assess the applications and to 'mark' the pedigrees out of 20. At the end of April begins the 'field work', the inspection of yearlings on the studs. Visits are planned with military precision. A map of Britain is posted with miniature flags denoting the studs which have entered yearlings, as well as those which have not but which should have done. The directors, and some less senior auctioneers, are assigned various groups of studs, county by county and throughout Ireland. Inspections are left until as late as possible, and often a second visit is arranged in the week after Royal Ascot. 'If we find fault in a yearling, breeders will say: "Come back later, and we'll have it right." What they mean is that if a foot turns out they will try to correct it with the help of their blacksmith. But it is a purely cosmetic device. You will invariably find that the following year, in training, the foot reverts to the original.'

At the end of the stud visits, the travelling assessors will file their reports, with a further mark out of 20. These are married with the pedigree assessments and the top 300 yearlings are chosen. In July the official entry forms are sent out to gather information such as owners' VAT status and the yearlings'

Ian Balding has bid 130,000 guineas. The bill to American owner Mr Paul Mellon will be $221,130 + VAT.

Trainer Paul Cole inspects a yearling at the Highflyer Paddock boxes. A well-bred, attractive
yearling could be 'pulled out' up to 50 or 60 times a day.

The ring. All agents have their favourite bidding areas, while the 'judges' – bidders who will buy a bargain on spec – hover around the entrance rope.

first-generation pedigree details. These details are fed into the internationally-linked Weatherby's computer which provides complete up-to-date pedigree details. 'If a pedigree is too long to fit on a single page of the catalogue it is edited to size. The computer indicates with a cut-off line exactly the limit of the space available. Page proofs are sent to the vendor, who can make any changes. Finally, the catalogue is printed in early September. The next stage is a promotion tour to market the sale.'

A week or so before the sale, the various auctioneers are delegated the specific lots that they are to sell. They sell ten horses at a time, which takes up to half an hour, and then move away from the rostrum for the next auctioneer to take over. 'When we receive our list, the first thing I do is to "mark up" – that's to say, research who bought the previous progeny of the mare, and for how much. That helps me to target a possible buyer. The horses arrive up to a week in advance – some of them need special treatment – but I don't inspect the horses I am selling until 24 hours before the sale. Most vendors like to discuss their yearlings and emphasise their best qualities.'

The advantage of a restricted sale is that there are enough boxes to accommodate every lot without yearlings having to be moved out and in. None-

'Don't leave me now!' Auctioneer David Pim defies a bidder to walk away. Press box critics
include Sue Montgomery, Tony Morris and bespectacled Tom Forrest.

theless, the organisation during sales week is intense. As well as permanent
paddock staff – repair men, gardeners, carpenters, painters – there are 121
'casuals' backed up by Securicor and a special security group. 'The problems
are endless. Invariably certain people are upset with their boxes. Then there
are arguments over whether or not a horse 'makes a noise'. Nowadays, we recommend that all horses come to the sales with a wind certificate signed within
21 days. The purchaser can retest the animal within 24 hours of the sale. If he
is not satisfied he can demand an examination by a panel of three vets whose
chairman is Professor Jeffrey Lane, the top expert in this field. If they find that
the horse is wrong in the wind, the sale is void.'

Another safeguard for buyers is the statutory indentity inspection, against
the yearling's passport. This is designed to avoid repetition of a recent cause
célèbre where two foals were confused on an Irish stud; the 'wrong' horse was
bought as a foal, sold on as a yearling and eventually raced for two seasons

The eye of the 'spotter'. Tattersalls employ attractive, sharp-eyed girls to assist the auctioneers in locating bidders.

When a horse walks out of the sale ring he steps into a new world – often halfway across the world.

before the error was discovered. The eventual purchaser was awarded damages of over £80,000. Nowadays, in the event of doubt, a blood test is taken and analysed at the nearby Animal Health Trust. 'Most of the disputes are settled amicably. Stable vices, like crib biting and wind sucking, must be declared from the rostrum. If a new bidder comes into the ring, you must repeat: "This horse has been seen to crib bite ..." Box walking and weaving do not have to be declared.

'Occasionally we have a disputed bid, but not too often. It usually happens when there are two bidders, one behind the other. The auctioneer will take the bid of the man in front and the "spotter" will take a simultaneous bid from the man behind. We've got dozens of spotters and they do a good job. But the system can go wrong. If there *is* a disputed bid, we restart the auction from the final bid. As an auctioneer, one aims to be familiar with every bidder. It's a cash business. If people establish that they can pay for a horse, we give them credit.

The shadows lengthen over Park Paddocks. Tattersalls' threat to quit Newmarket and move to the Irish Republic was inspired by the imbalance of VAT rates between Britain and Ireland.

Over the years we have had very few defaulters. The problems are usually occasioned by agents who take on a client without sufficient research into his credit-worthiness. Tattersalls are simply not in a position to check it out. If the client cannot, or will not, pay, then everyone is in deep trouble.'

Such an episode occurred in 1987 with a new overseas client of a reputable Newmarket-based bloodstock agency. Tattersalls' eventual short-fall was in excess of £150,000. 'We take a lot of trouble over credit-worthiness. We pay out to vendors on the 28th day after the sale, regardless of whether we have been paid by the purchaser – unless, of course, there has been a dispute'.

Mildmay-White and his colleagues are invariably exhausted by the second week of December. 'There are seven sales in quick succession. Fairyhouse, the Highflyer, the October Open, the Horses-In-Training, the November, the Fairyhouse November and finally the December Sales. At one stage we are selling horses four weeks out of five. Then we have to try to collect the money!'

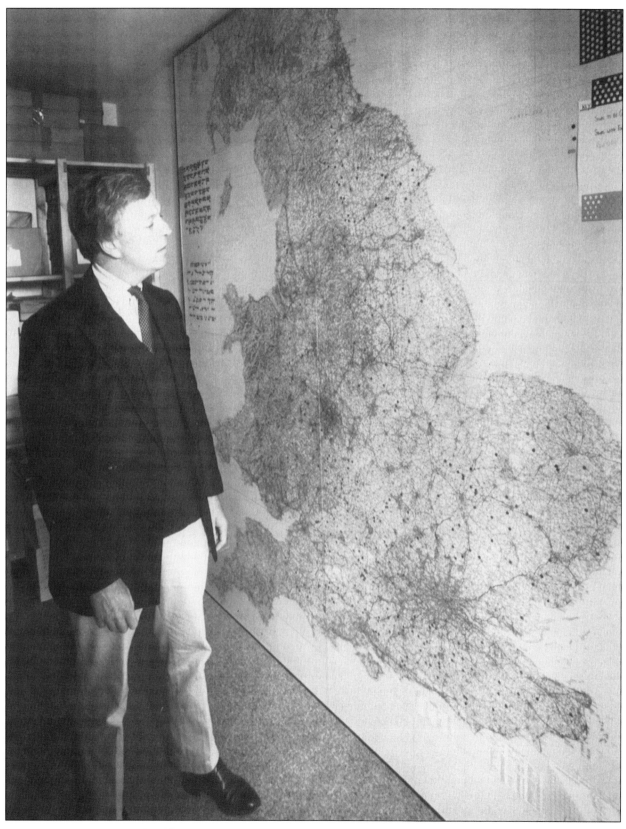

'General' Mildmay-White plans a campaign to visit all UK studs with yearling sale entries.
Studs are visited – and revisited – between April and June.

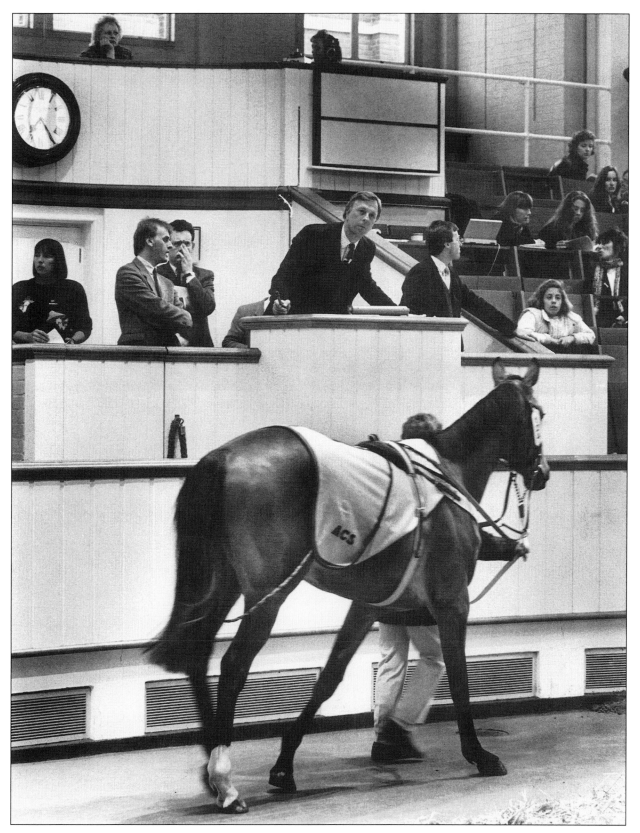

'Auctioneering is in the blood. You don't *make* auctioneers…' Mildmay-White elicits a bid at
the Horses-in-Training Sale.

But Mildmay-White, who lives near Bury St. Edmunds with his attractive wife Sara and three children aged 12, ten and two and a half, loves the life. 'I enjoy the selling … seeing the yearlings … and seeing the people. It gives you a great buzz. I admit I am nervous beforehand. If you stop feeling nervous, you have lost it. Even the smallest sale is important.

'Auctioneering is in the blood. You don't *make* auctioneers … it's part of your make-up. Everyone has their bad days. I had a frightful row with Humphrey Cottrill once over a late bid. He was simply furious but I know I was right. Two days later he apologised and we've been friends since. There is one day I will always remember. I sold a filly called Tenea. She was the first horse to be sold for £1 million in Europe. It was quite a moment. She was led up by a lad called Roy Collins. Tattersalls give £1 in the thousand to the lad leading up, from our 5 per cent commission. Roy Collins went off with £1000 in his pocket. I don't know how much he had left by the time he got home!'

The Trainer

Ian Balding

Ian Balding's summer day begins at 5 a.m. He slips out of bed trying, without success, not to disturb his wife Emma and creaks down to the kitchen to make tea. Pollie (lurcher), Lilly (boxer) and Taggie (border terrier) are pushed out of the back door, and the day's first serious task begins.

The Slate

This entails matching 80-odd horses with available riders, over two lots. During the season some horses and personnel will invariably be away. Balding

In the presence of greatness. Balding's two-year-olds take a turn past the statue of Mill Reef.

The slate. Balding struggles to match the available riders with two lots of horses. Already prepared is the gallop sheet (foreground). On work mornings Balding records every gallop in his work book.

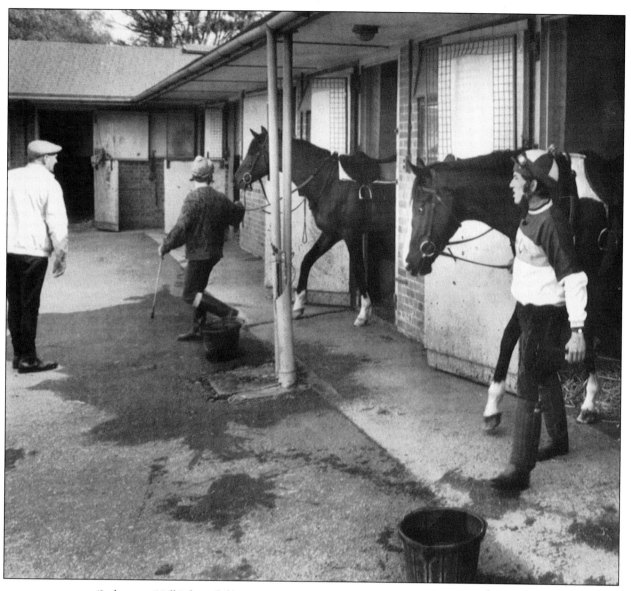

'Jockeys out!' Bill Palmer (left) summons second lot. John Matthias (now in Hong Kong) leads out Secret Silence.

matches man with horse, and conveys the slate to the stable yard before the staff arrive at 5.45. The 'work' list on galloping days (Wednesday and Saturday) takes rather longer to accomplish and is usually prepared overnight. Balding talks to his head man, Bill Palmer, returns to the house, collects the dogs, bundles them in the back of his station wagon and sets out to inspect the gallops. It is now 6 a.m.

Kingsclere has two principal gallops. Hollowshot, in the valley, is the winter ground but is also used during the summer for light exercise. Watership Down – the inspiration for Richard Adams's bestseller – is the summer gallop, high on the Berkshire downs. Balding inspects the turf, evaluating the effect of rain or drought and alert for miscreant moles, and returns to Park House for a quick glance at the *Sporting Life* and a second cup of tea.

At 52, Balding, riding Experimenting, remains fit for point-to-points, hunter chases and team chasing.

At 6.50 the impressive first lot pull out of the yard, coats gleaming and hooves clattering. Balding rides out on a stable hack and, as the string threads its way towards the downs, moves up from horse to horse giving specific orders to each lad. On arrival, after 20 minutes' walking, the horses jog around for five minutes, sort themselves into the prescribed twos and threes, and set off on their first three-furlong canter. This completed, they return to the assembly ring, before peeling off to their set-off points for the main work – either five furlongs, six furlongs, seven furlongs, or one mile. The horses to be galloped do a gentle canter to the top of the hill, switch their riders for jockeys or senior work riders, and return to the bottom. Now the serious work begins under Balding's eagle eye. As the horses flash by Balding's hack at the top of the gallop, the trainer makes a quick assessment as to whether each horse is an imminent runner and possible winner.

'There's a monster in there…' Secret Silence, ears pricked, is determined to find something to
shy at – bird, beast or bumble bee!

Breakfast with Balding. Champion lady jockey Clare Balding goes to work on a slice of melon. The trainer confers with jockey, vet, wife and assistant.

Back at Park House, breakfast is eaten in the kitchen between 8.30 and 9. Balding's intake is half a grapefruit, toast and coffee. 'When owners come – notably George Strawbridge – Emma gives us a cooked breakfast. Otherwise we have to make do,' Balding complains. 'In spring and autumn, when the horses go out later, we don't have breakfast until 9.30 – and that's a nightmare. The telephone never stops ringing … I don't have time to talk to my jockeys … and declarations have to be done by 10. In the summer we can discuss the work quietly; my secretary arrives at 9 a.m. and by then we're well ahead.'

The second lot horses leave the yard at 9.40. Some may be exercised on the horse-walker (a mechanical walking device) and some may swim in Balding's private horse pool. Balding sees them out of the yard and then prepares to go racing.

The Races

Balding eases into the driving seat of his Citroën CX GTI Turbo; checks the presence of raceglasses and trainer's badge, and directs the fast car towards the day's major race meeting. It is a well-worn path. Within a quarter of an hour he remembers at least one important thing that he has forgotten to check with his secretary. A carphone is now an intrinsic part of a racing man's life.

At the races, Balding heads straight for the weighing room to ensure that his runners have been declared by travelling head man 'Spider' Hackney. If one of his runners is either an important or nervous horse, he will go to the racecourse stables to check his condition. From the stables he walks onto the racecourse. 'I love to have a walk on the track before racing, either to check the going, or to accompany an apprentice jockey. It can sometimes help. I can tell an apprentice: "Don't go on the inside – it looks really rough." One usually learns something, and I like doing it. I always walk round if I'm riding myself. [Balding, at 52, still rides in point-to-points and hunter chases.] You always learn a little bit more about a racecourse.

Secret Silence (John Matthias) leads two stable-companions on the woodchip gallop. The colt was one of the stable's most promising two-year-olds until he sustained a minor injury.

Out on his own: Secret Silence sparkles in his work. The rolling downs at Kingsclere are in stark contrast to Newmarket's flat heathland.

'Sometimes I'll say to my jockey: "I'm quite certain it'll be faster on the strips they have rolled." If the grass is long, and it has been rolled, it can make a considerable difference to be racing on a strip that has been rolled in the direction the horses are running. After walking the course I'll go to the bar for a coffee and sandwich. I don't bet, and I don't drink on the racecourse, so my mind is uncluttered.

'I'm very meticulous about saddling. I can't remember being responsible for a saddle slipping. I won't let a starter go near my jockey's girths. We use a rubber undercoat beneath the saddle and elastic girths both sides, so nine times out of ten there is no need to adjust them. Personally, I think horses are overgirthed. The rubber we use nowadays is very soft. In the olden days it was indented like a ping-pong bat and horses were very sore afterwards.

'When my jockey comes into the paddock, he'll probably say, "Such and such is fancied." And I'll say, "Right – track that one." I always impress upon jockeys that they shouldn't hesitate to go on if there's no gallop. If a jockey is riding a two-year-old for me first time out I'll say, "This is a nice horse ... he's a bit green. He's OK at the stalls, win if you can – but he's not ready for a hard race."

A perfect summer's morning. Secret Silence enjoys a light snack while John Matthias
briefs the trainer.

Autumn leaves: the mornings become cooler and coats begin to change. Second lot relax after
morning exercise.

Time for a break. John Matthias vaults off Secret Silence after morning exercise.

'Then it's off to the grandstand. I like to get as high up as I can to read the race properly. Luckily I've got a super pair of raceglasses from Mappin and Webb. I form my own view of a race and the jockey fills in the details.

'After my last runner, I go straight home. There will always be either my jockey, an apprentice, or my daughter Clare to drive me. I telephone any absent owners on the carphone – I tend to convey good news to owners rather quicker than bad news! – and then I fall fast asleep.

'When we've been at the local or metropolitan meetings, I aim to get back by evening stables, between 5.30 and 6.30. I look round the horses, talk to Bill Palmer about lame horses and those that won't eat, and then it's time for more telephoning. In the summer, if it's a nice evening, we'll play tennis after stables. My brother Toby, John Francome and my family all make up a good foursome. In the winter I'll play squash, or go running for a couple of miles. We have dinner between 8 and 9 p.m. I really hate people ringing up during dinner. When a day is as busy as ours, it's lovely to get through your meal uninterrupted.

'Call this "Good to Firm"?' Balding sticks his heel into the resilient Goodwood turf and reflects
on orders for Seamus O'Gorman.

An apprehensive swimmer, accompanied by the human equivalent of water wings, faces the ramp to the pool.

'I thought I was bred to win the Derby – not swim the Channel!' A fit horse can complete up to ten circuits. More is inadvisable.

The horse-walker is safe, labour-saving and can move in either direction. But it is not universally popular.

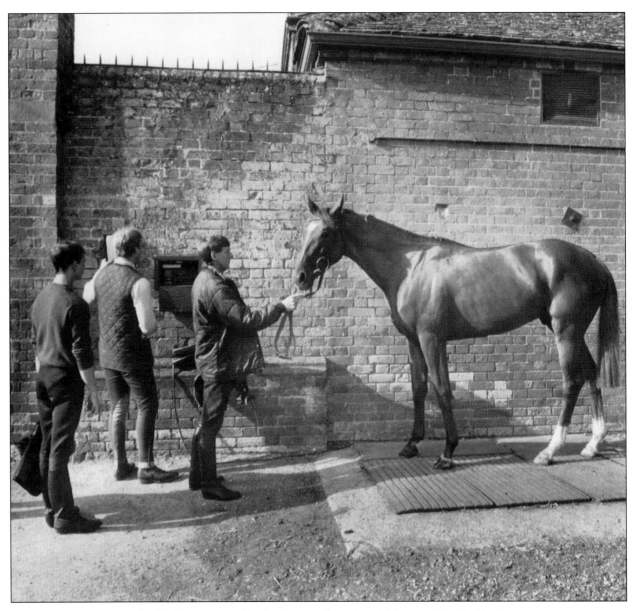

Weight check. A two-year-old colt steps onto the scales while assistant Patrick Chamings checks for weight variation. The average two-year-old weighs 450 kilos.

'After dinner I may watch a movie on TV – I'm a glutton for bad movies. At 11 p.m. I come alive again. This is when I telephone my American owners. Then I do my work list and possibly get to bed about one in the morning. When things are going well it's easy to keep going. But you can understand why some trainers go off the rails in July and August.

'We never get a holiday in the summer. We spend two days away at York for the Ebor meeting [mid-August], and five days at the sales in Keeneland during July. That's far from a holiday! It's hard work and extremely hot. We also have a week at Saratoga which is more relaxed. During the winter we go skiing for two weeks with the kids [Clare and Andrew], but most of the spring I spend point-to-pointing.'

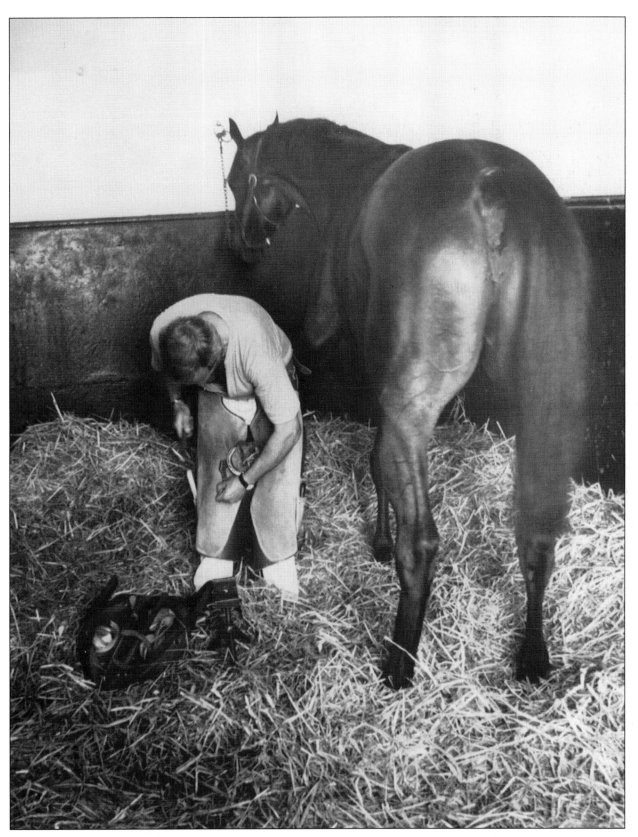

A trip to the races means a change of footwear. The blacksmith fits light aluminium racing plates in place of the heavier, more resilient work shoes.

The stables at Kingsclere date back to the 1860s. John Porter, their first occupant, trained three winners of the Triple Crown – Ormonde, Common and Flying Fox – and built the top yard in 1888.

Balding grew up in the saddle. His father, Gerald Balding, was regarded as the best Englishman ever to play polo – one of the very few ten-goal players in the history of the sport. He captained England for years. 'My brother [Toby] and I played polo as kids, but sadly had to give up when father died,' Balding reflects. After the war, Gerald Balding trained a string of mostly National Hunt racehorses at Bishop's Cannings. In 1953 he moved to Weyhill where Toby, the older of the brothers, still trains.

'I was thrust onto racehorses at the age of ten,' Balding recalls. 'I remember being terrified of them. But when I was 15 it suddenly became quite fun. I rode in my first race at the age of 16, on a horse called The Quiet Man. My father had ensured that he remained a maiden [non-winner] all season, so he could find a bad race for him and have a "touch". He had surprising faith in me! Unfortunately he chose a race at Fakenham, a course that he had never visited. The Quiet Man was a long-striding horse and, unbeknown to my father, Fakenham, of course, is like the Wall of Death! In the end we finished third, to a horse ridden by Lord Manton. Next time out we went to Ludlow, but Dad had lost his nerve and didn't have a bet. We won at 20–1!'

Balding developed into one of the best post-war amateur riders and was beaten by a single winner by Sir William Pigott-Brown for the amateurs' title in 1962-63. Inevitably there was pressure on him to turn professional, but fate intervened. His future father-in-law, Captain Peter Hastings-Bass, telephoned the aspiring jockey in the spring of 1964 with the exciting invitation: 'Come and be my assistant trainer.' Within three months of Balding's arrival at Kingsclere, Peter Hastings died. The 25-year-old assistant took out a temporary licence, took over the string and has never looked back. In 1969 he married

Balding's tack-room boasts the colours of some of the world's leading owners: HM The Queen, The Queen Mother, Mr Paul Mellon and Sheikh Mohammed.

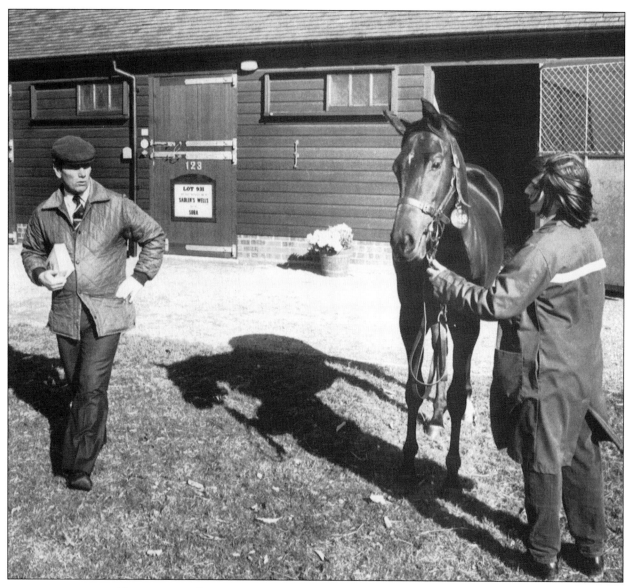

Balding examines a filly by Sharpo at the October Open Sales. Impressed, he bought her for 19,000 guineas.

Emma Hastings-Bass and in 1970 there arrived in the yard a horse called Mill Reef.

Balding remains an active and competitive sportsman, with a brilliant eye for a ball. At riding, cricket, tennis, squash and skiing he continues to excel. But his greatest sporting skill was rugby union. He played full-back for Cambridge University for three years, winning his Blue with the famous unbeaten XV of 1960-61. It was a side that boasted nine internationals including Brian Thomas, Mike Wade and Gordon Waddell. The Oxford team included John Wilcox, Richard Sharp and the legendary American, Peter Dawkins, the man who introduced the torpedo throw to British rugby. Balding's best friends remain his 'rugger chums', including the former Scottish international, now broadcaster, Ian Robertson.

Measuring the height of a yearling. Rough guide: if you are 5ft 10in tall and the bridge of your nose is parallel to the horse's withers, he stands 16.1hh.

Balding is phlegmatic about the future. 'What I love about training is the healthy, active, outdoor life. I consider myself exceptionally lucky to have lived and worked somewhere as beautiful as Kingsclere. I'm never more grateful to be here than when I've had a bad day – everything has gone wrong, horses have run disappointingly – and I can come home, walk the dogs on the training grounds, and be completely private.

'I used to feel that the successes we have heavily outweigh the many, many disappointments, but now, with all the hassles of life, I'm not so sure. The burden of running a major business, a large property, and training 80 horses can be quite oppressive.

Stable lads' boxing is one of racing's great traditions. Balding invariably fields a strong team for the National Championships. The finals are held at the Hilton in November.

The end of the beginning. Three years and three months after his birth, Secret Silence makes
his first appearance on a racecourse, in May 1991. So far he has cost his owner over $250,000.
The Kempton prize was £3,125. He finished seventh.

'Now my main ambition is to have the opportunity to *buy* Kingsclere [at
the moment it belongs to the McDougald family – one of Balding's owners]
and to hand over to my son Andrew in ten years' time. That would be a very
satisfactory life's achievement.'

The Head Lad

Bill Palmer

The position of head lad in a racing stable is not so much a job as a way of life. A hard way of life. Bill Palmer, head lad to Ian Balding at Kingsclere, works a 60-hour week, from dawn – 5 a.m. during summer – until the end of evening stables at 7 p.m. After 22 years he is now one of racing's longest-serving head lads. It is a status that he hopes to maintain until retirement.

Feed time. Palmer sifts a bowl of corn as the lads wait for horses' breakfasts to be served. The lad names the horse to be fed so Palmer can adjust the measure accordingly.

Bill Palmer keeps an eye on the *Racing Post*, and an ear on the radio, as he prepares blindfold
and quoits for starting-stalls practice.

Long reining. After two days of getting used to wearing tack, the yearlings move on to the long reining stage, learning the riders' signals to turn left and right.

A good big one and a good little 'un. Mill Reef, who never grew beyond 15.2hh, looks on as the robust Secret Silence is driven by Bill Palmer.

'To be honest, there is not a great deal else I could do,' smiles Bill. 'When I was younger, I was ambitious to do well for myself – perhaps to train. Now, I'm happy enough just to work with horses. I'm not mechanically-minded, or electrically-minded – and I certainly can't mend a fuse!'

Bill's dawn duty is to go round the 80-odd horses to check that everything is normal. There could be horses cast (wedged against the box wall); coughing; or even kidnapped! Unlike many yards, Balding's horses do not have an early morning feed. At 6 a.m. in the summer, the lads arrive to muck out and prepare their horses for first lot. Bill will bustle around the yard helping to fasten bandages and boots on vulnerable horses and attending to general duties. The head lad is the sergeant-major and directly responsible for the conduct and capabilities of the 'men'.

At 6.50 first lot pulls out of the yard and on to the beautiful rolling Berkshire downs. When the weather is good, this is the best part of the day. Unlike many head lads, Bill rides out both lots of horses. 'I love riding out – I'd be lost if I didn't. I couldn't bear just to stay lungeing. I like to see what's going on.'

A quick check of the stable rota and the running plans for the week. Most lads and girls look after three horses.

At 8.30, as first lot returns, Bill busies himself with checking nicks and cuts from the morning's exercise and dressing any wounds. Then the 40-odd first lot horses are fed. 'Feeding is one job that is easier nowadays. Twenty years ago we would feed mostly scotch oats, barley and chaff. The oats would need to be shaken to get the dust out, you would bruise your own barley, and then boil it, while the chaff cutter was manually operated. Nowadays, we use a complete feed mix – oats, maize, soya beans, wheat and barley, all in a compound mixture, with syrup as an appetiser. We still have one linseed mash a week, on Saturday evening. Some people feed horse nuts, but we don't use them.'

After the horses' breakfast comes Bill's breakfast, whereupon the entire cycle begins again for second lot. These horses pull out of the yard at 9.40 and return, to be fed, at 11.30. The lunch break comes around midday. 'Personally, I have nothing to eat. In the afternoon, I will play golf, mess around in the garden, or watch racing on TV. I can't understand people who sleep during the day. I go to bed at eleven and get up at five and that's quite enough sleep for me.'

Evening stables begin at 4.30. 'I go round the horses feeling their legs, making sure they have eaten up, and checking their skin for warbles and ringworm. The guv'nor comes round at 5.30 and I walk around with him for part of the way. Then I hive off to do the evening feed. The day ends at around 7 p.m. but I am always on duty. With horses an emergency is never far away.'

Bill has been used to life with horses for as long as he can remember. Born in a village called Mary Tavy, on the edge of Dartmoor, Bill was the son of Frederick Palmer, a hill farmer with a smallholding of 150 acres. Bill grew up amongst the sheep, cattle and ponies grazing on the moors, and began riding ponies at a very early age, soon graduating to gymkhanas. At the age of 14 he left home to work at Kingsbridge, Devon for local horseman Tom Jarvis, who prepared point-to-pointers and sold them on to be National Hunt horses. The following year, in 1948, he moved on to become apprentice to the gentleman trainer Gerald Balding, at Bishop's Cannings, near Devizes, Wiltshire. In those days an apprenticeship lasted five years, and Bill's pay was 5s (25p) a week for the first six months; 7s 6d (37½p) a week for the next three months; whereafter he received the princely sum of 15s (75p). After three years his pay was increased to £1 a week, with 'keep'.

His first ride was in a two-mile steeplechase at Leicester on 8 January 1952. The horse was called Old Kentucky and was owned by the American Mr Jock Whitney. His first winner eventually came at the now defunct Buckfastleigh in August the same year on a horse called Paricutin. 'He was a grand old horse, owned by Lord Stavordale. His lordship came to me afterwards and was delighted. "Well done, Palmer," he said, "I'd like you to have these." My present was a brace of partridge.'

At the age of 19, Bill was called up to do his National Service. He spent two years in the RAF and returned at the end of it still weighing just 9st 7lb. Since then, with the exception of one year when he went to ride for Reg Withycombe at Henley-on-Thames, Bill has worked for a member of the Balding family.

The first steps down the long road to becoming a racehorse. A private estate like Kingsclere is
the ideal scenario for early education.

Bill Palmer fits the long reins to the snaffle in readiness for the next stage of
Secret Silence's education.

Ridden away. Secret Silence, having completed his lungeing and long reining, is ridden for the first time. The 'hardware' includes a Fulmer breaking bridle, standing martingale, side reins and brushing boots.

'Mr Balding had moved to Weyhill while I was away. I was getting a few rides, but the job at Withycombe's sounded more attractive. Then I met Mr Balding at Worcester one day and he said: "Bill, come back." I did and I have never regretted it. Sadly, Mr Balding died 12 months later, in 1957, and Toby took over the licence. He was just 21 at the time, but he gave me a chance and I never looked back.'

Bill rode 90-odd winners over the following 10 years, including Green Light in the Princess Royal Hurdle – a horse he also rode in the Champion

Hurdle. As the door closed on his riding career in 1969, a new door opened with the offer to become head lad to Toby's brother Ian. Bill started work at Kingsclere on 15 December. Two months earlier a small bay yearling colt had arrived in the yard. He was called Mill Reef. 'That was a great time for the yard, but it was a hard act to follow,' Bill reflects wryly. 'But once you've worked with a horse like that, you always *hope* that another one will come along.

'Those were good days, in the early 1970s. Sadly, a lot of things have gone downhill since then. The lads, especially. The trainers should have given them a decent pay rise 20 years ago, to keep the good ones in racing. Instead they drifted away to work at Aldermaston, Harwell and places like that. They'll never come back now. A lot of Lambourn lads have gone off to work in the tile factory at Benham – £200 a week, and a five-day week. What chance have you got? Mind you, we're very lucky here in that we have 15 married lads, with kids, who don't want to move away from Kingsclere. The guv'nor looks after them very well. Unlike many yards, we've only got a handful of girls. They're kind to horses, but ...

'It's very sad to see racing go downhill in so many ways. In my opinion, all-weather racing has totally degraded the sport.'

But the depression of a dull, dry August, with horses coughing, jarred up and brutally exposed as mediocre, invariably turns to optimism as the new intake arrive in the autumn. 'It's always an exciting time. The yearlings come either from the sales or from private studs. By and large, I prefer the sales yearlings. They have always been well handled, and know the basics. Mr [Paul] Mellon's home-bred horses go to Yorkshire as foals, and sometimes they are as wild as hawks when they come back!'

Secret Silence embraced the best of both worlds when he arrived at Kingsclere. He was owned by Mr Mellon – who has only the best – but was bought at the Newmarket Highflyer Sales, for which he had been meticulously prepared. The education of the yearlings is undertaken by Bill and another senior lad, 'Spider' Hackney.

'We start off by lungeing the yearlings in the indoor school, going both ways. They do that for a few days. When they are going kindly enough, we put the tack on. After a couple of days in tack, we move on to the long reins. We drive them in long reins for about a week, ending up with doing circles, and eventually we drag them through the stalls, so they are used to everything. Then we put the jockey up, and they are ridden away. It all takes about 14 days. A lot of people do it quicker, but we like to take our time.

'Of course accidents do happen. One horse on long reins got loose one day and went a mile down the road to Kingsclere, long reins flapping, and traffic scattering! Eventually we caught him, and there wasn't a scratch on him. Of course, he turned out to be no good. Dashing Blade did something similar one day, avoiding cars like a fly-half. Surprisingly, he *did* turn out to be pretty good.

'After they are ridden away, they go out to the paddock to learn their figure-of-eights, and then move on to the hack. After a few days they canter up the gallops behind a lead horse ... the lads get a bit braver and shorten their stirrups, and eventually the yearlings move on to canter upsides. Once they've been upsides we leave them alone, and don't do a lot more until the end of February. Now they start to go a bit faster, and gradually we increase the workload. They do more upsides work and quicken the pace. After a few bits of work, we know what's what. It's always exciting our first day up on the downs. Until then the preparatory work is all done in the valley.

'Mind you, we are always a little behind most people up here. It's usually the end of April before we really push on. Spring is the best time of the year. We are all full of hope. Everything is starting to happen. The three-year-olds are coming on, and you hope they may have improved, and the two-year-olds are starting to show something.

'The cold weather has destroyed the germs, and the horses are healthy. Of course, you're always in dread of "the virus". It's very often an excuse for bad horses. But horses *do* get sick. We had a terrible year for virus in 1972 – I'll never forget it. We've had a few bad gos since, but nothing as bad as that. The only thing to do when you've got sick horses is to give them a complete rest.

'There has probably always been a virus, or something akin to it. When I was an apprentice, the stable would go through a bad spell and we would say: "They haven't come to themselves … they need some sun on their backs." In truth, they had drippy noses, but we didn't know how to deal with the problem. Nowadays, I read a lot of veterinary books, and try to maximise our precautions.'

Bill Palmer was 58 on 27 February. He and his wife Annie have been married for 34 years. Their son, Gerald, is a surveyor in Warwick ('He was always too big for racing'). Of their two daughters, Cecilia and Clare, one is married, and the other is a sister at Basingstoke Hospital.

Horses, and racing, remain Bill's whole life. 'I've enjoyed it. I wouldn't change it very much. There are times when things are not going very well – bad horses, bad weather during the winter – and you get a bit down. But then the spring comes, something wins a decent race and everyone is alive again. Success is a great pick-me-up.

'I enjoy having the responsibility of the yard. It's all down to me, and I am answerable only to the guv'nor. I've made a good living out of the game. I don't want to be rich – I've got enough for a rainy day.

'Yes, I'm happy. I'll certainly go on until I feel I'm not wanted.'

The Stable Lad

John Wilkinson

The racing game is for many a fantasy world, built on dreams. Some rich men try to buy 'the dream' – occasionally with success. For the rest, racing is an endless search for the rainbow's end … that one Good Horse. John Wilkinson has always had 'the dream'. At first he dreamed of becoming a top flat-race

Brush and curry comb. John Wilkinson grooms the apprehensive newcomer. Thoroughbreds are invariably ticklish and a wise groom keeps an eye on the near hind leg for a sudden cow-kick.

A trip to the barn. A horse's bed will have fresh straw added each day.

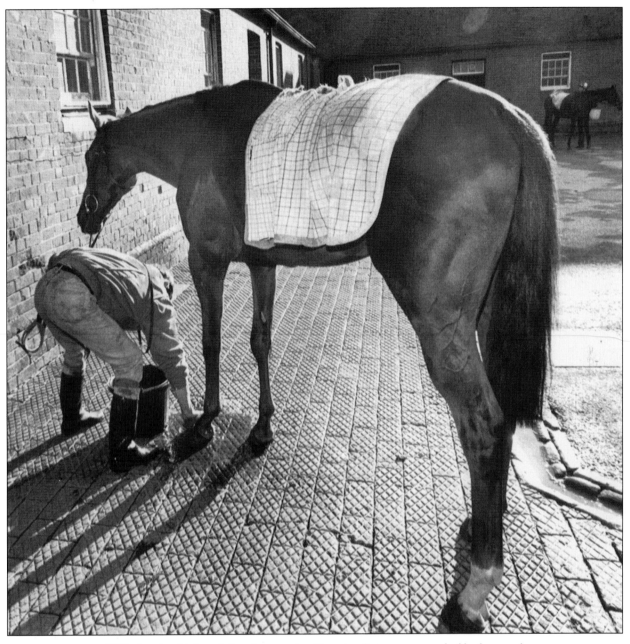

'Wilky' washes his horse's feet after exercise. Lingering dirt can cause cracked heels or mud fever. Hooves are oiled for evening stables.

jockey – famous and rich. Then, as his weight increased and success eluded him, his dream reshaped itself into an ambition to become a giant of the jumping game.

Now, almost 30 years after his first hesitant steps into racing, the original dream has become an unlikely mirage – a quest to become a racehorse trainer … 'Winner trained by J. Wilkinson.' … The daily reality is the conscientious, and sometimes monotonous, care of three valuable flat-race thoroughbreds trained by Ian Balding. Amongst them in 1991 was Mr Paul Mellon's colt Secret Silence.

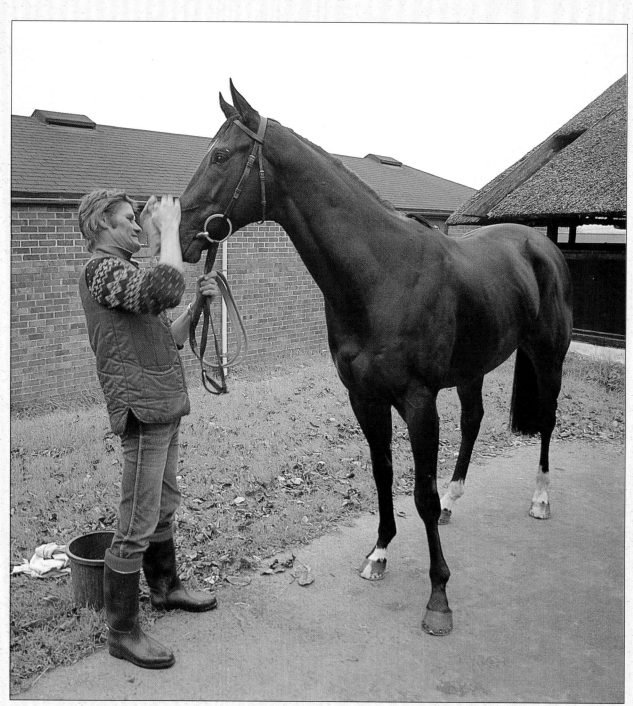

Another important part of the grooming routine: keeping the horse's nose clean.

John Wilkinson was born into the coal mining community around Gateshead, in the industrial north-east. His father worked in the Marley Hill pit, seven miles from Gateshead, which was closed in June 1963. Isaac Wilkinson was made redundant and never worked again. John left Dunstan Secondary Modern School aged 15 and, reacting positively to the limitations of his shape and size – he measured 4ft 11in and weighed 5st 7lb – he determined to become a jockey. He travelled south to the stables of R. J. (Jack) Colling at

West Ilsley and entered a five-year apprenticeship. 'It was very hard,' John recalls. 'We apprentices lived in a wooden shack – you couldn't call it anything else – and earned ten shillings a week. In the winter it was bitterly cold. The downs were bleak and I felt a long way from home.

'I was always hoping to get some rides, but it never happened. Once, in September 1964, I was supposed to ride a horse called Dicey in an apprentice race at Ascot, but they thought that I wouldn't be able to "do" the weight, so another apprentice, Geoff Parkes, got the ride.'

In 1966, after five long and austere years, John accepted the inevitable. There was no chance that he would ever become a flat-race jockey. 'So I decided to try my hand at jumping. I went to Hawick in Scotland to work for Mr Kenneth Oliver. It was a stable that was enjoying terrific success.

'I was there on and off for nine years, and I was given my chance. I rode 13 winners from about 140 rides. Mind you, there was plenty of competition for rides. Barry Brogan, Tommy Stack and Peter Ennis were all riding for the stable. But luckily there were plenty of good horses to go round. The best horse that I rode was October, who I looked after. He won the three-mile handicap hurdle at Ayr at the New Year Meeting two years running and I rode him both times.'

The Hon Jane Weir, whose husband George owned October, recalls: 'John was a super lad and looked after October all the time that he was with the Olivers. The horse was a credit to him. He knew the horse well; schooled him; and the rides were a "thank you" for his hard work.'

'I suppose I was quite lucky with injuries,' John recalls. 'My worst fall was at Ayr on a horse called Auchentibber, in November 1969. He bolted on the way to the start and buried me at the first. I fractured a rib and punctured a lung. I made my comeback at Catterick six weeks later, on New Year's Eve, on a horse called Denholm in a novices' chase. He won – and I was written up by Peter O'Sullevan!

'In the end I wasn't riding so many and I decided to move on. I was supposed to go to Joe Mulhall at York, but I changed my mind and ended up with Bobby Hall at Newcastle. I stayed there for a season, and had ten or 12 rides, but I was going with a girl who worked for Harry Bell at Hawick. It was only 60 miles away, but the obvious thing was to move back to Hawick. We got married in July 1971. I went to work for Mr Bell, but that didn't last long and I ended up going back to Mr Oliver.'

Ironically, marriage heralded the end of the beginning for John Wilkinson. David Moorhead and Colin Tinkler were now riding most of the horses trained by Ken Oliver and rides became few and far between. John struck a bad patch. His father died, and his marriage disintegrated. Suddenly his world was falling apart. Disillusioned, like so many others who have grabbed at 'the dream' but felt it slip through their fingers like a wriggling trout, John decided to turn his back on racing.

His first job outside was driving a fork-lift truck in a chemical factory. Later, he worked with beer barrels on a trading estate in Gateshead. His shift-work pay was £116 a week. As a stableman he had received just half of that.

A day at the races is the icing on the cake. Every lad enjoys 'leading up' – especially if the race is on TV. Secret Silence has run a pleasing race.

Within 12 months John had married for the second time. This marriage yielded two children, a son Richard born in July 1977 and a daughter Lianne born in December 1979. In the 1980s John felt the urge to move back into racing.

'There was no work in the north-east and, yes, I was missing working with horses. I couldn't stand being on the dole. I don't know how people can do that. I got a job working for Peter Haynes who had started training five miles outside Chichester when Derek Kent left to go to Hong Kong. It was a good job. I was driving the horsebox and I had responsibility. What's more they served a good pint of Webster's Yorkshire bitter in the local pub!'

Sadly, the effects of an equine virus forced Peter Haynes out of business and the job came to an end. 'So I had to look round once again. I knew a couple of lads who worked for Ian Balding, so here I am. Back where I started – in a flat-racing stable in Berkshire.'

John's day begins at 6 a.m. and his morning duties finish at 11.30. Evening stables last from 4.30 to 6.30. He works alternate weekends. His job as a groom is a cross between valet, masseur and hairdresser. 'My first job in the morning, at 6.30, is to muck out my first two horses. Then I dress them over and put the tack on the horse that I'm riding first lot. When we get back from exercise, I brush my horse down; sponge out the girth marks; and make him comfortable. If it's muddy, I'll wash his feet outside the box door. I use a light sponge for his eyes, and a dandy brush to groom his mane and tail.

'Unfortunately, because it's a flat-race yard, I don't get to ride much fast work. I'm too heavy at 10st 4lb. So I just ride educational work. I do miss it.

'It's not a bad life. I like my pint at the weekend – anyone will tell you that! I use the local club – the Peter and Paul Club – it belongs to the church. The beer is quite cheap. Nowadays I drink Double Diamond. Sadly, my second wife and I are apart, but I feel I'm getting my act together. I've a niece from Newcastle who looks after the kids. My wife lives in Evesham. They go there every other weekend.

'I take my holidays in Newcastle. I'll take a car, visit all the family, and see the lads that I used to work with. We'll all meet at Sunday lunchtime for a few beers – Exhibition … that's a proper beer that! One thing I'd love to do is to fly; I've never been in an aeroplane.

'I suppose the magic fades with the years. When you start off in racing you love your horses. But the longer you're in it, the more love turns to routine and it becomes just a profession. It's the dream of a Derby winner that keeps you going – that once-in-a-lifetime horse. Then it's all been worth it … your boat's come in.

'Mind you, I looked after some good horses in my time at West Ilsley. I "did" a horse called High Trees, owned by Mr Astor [now Sir John]. He won nine races as a four-year-old. Scobie Breasley got off him one day and said: "You'll never know how good he is – he never does a tap." One day Joe Mercer rode him at York and he came to the post four lengths clear. Right on the line he stuck his toes in and Joe went over his shoulder. They had to look at the photo finish to see if Joe landed before or after the line! He was a bit of a lad.

'I like my pint at the weekend – anyone will tell you that!' John Wilkinson enjoys a drink at
the Swan with his children, Richard and Lianne, looking on.

'And I rode work on Provoke – Major Hern had taken over the stable by then. I backed him when he won the St Leger from Meadow Court – at 50–1! I still like my bet at the weekend. If racing is on TV I will always have my 50p yankee. But I'm not a very lucky person at all.

'I do hope to become a trainer one day. If my boat came in with the football pools, that's what I would do. I'd find a place in Sussex, and train between 25 and 30 horses.

'I look after some nice horses at present. The guv'nor doesn't rush them. The Secretariat horse [Secret Silence] could be all right. He's very green at present, but he covers a lot of ground for a little horse. He's well-made and a lovely mover. And he's a very nice-natured horse. Of course he's bred to catch pigeons … Who knows? He might be the one …'

The Jockey

Steve Cauthen

Steve Cauthen's working day during the summer begins soon after dawn and often continues until almost midnight. Riding work for Newmarket trainer Clive Brittain means a 5 a.m. start. The horses gallop at 5.45. If there is an evening meeting at Goodwood, Wolverhampton, Pontefract or Newcastle, Steve will almost certainly be travelling home long after the trainers have

Steve weighs out, and presents his medical book to the Clerk of the Scales. A jockey weighs out with saddle, weight-cloth, felt or foam under saddle, blinkers and boots.

These boots were made for riding. The former champion zips on his handmade lightweight boots, in his personal corner of the old Newbury weighing room.

retired to bed. It is an exhausting schedule and not conducive to a stable diet. 'I can't eat until I finish riding, and in mid-summer the last race can be as late as 9.15. If I remember to, I'll take a few things with me – say, a couple of apples to eat after racing. When I get home, I'll have a light salad. Otherwise we might eat somewhere on the way home, but that makes it very late.'

Flat-racing weights demand that Steve keeps his masculine frame honed to sparse, bare minimum shape. The racing weight scale ranges from 10st to 7st 7lb. His two great rivals Pat Eddery and Willie Carson ride comfortably at 8st 4lb and 7st 11lb respectively. Carson even scaled 7st 7lb on one occasion in 1990. Steve has the greatest difficulty in reducing and maintaining his weight at 8st 7lb. It is a traditional problem for the flat-racing greats. Fred Archer's

The valets have been at work since early morning. They clean boots, breeches, saddles and waterproofs. Frankie Dettori (left) has checked his weight on the trial scales. The jockeys' changing room is the holy of holies.

'The touts won't see this one!' Belmez (Steve Cauthen) walks through Newmarket's
Racecourse Car Park towards the 'across-the-flat' gallop.

Dawn watch. Cauthen works the classic colt Belmez in the early morning mist, on
Newmarket's Racecourse Side.

starvation diet and drastic purgatives led to illness, manic depression and suicide at the age of 29. Lester Piggott, after a period of ballooning to 10st 7lb in the winter months, decided that stability was preferable to brief bouts of pleasure followed by deprivation and pain. So he stopped eating.

Steve has come to terms with the Piggott method. Until autumn 1985 he would dine in prestigious restaurants, and drink the best champagne and fine wines. It was the year that he rode a remarkable 195 domestic winners and won the Derby on Slip Anchor. He had driven his body to its limit and the effect was traumatic. He questioned the merit of sustaining his energy and drive for success with artificial stimulants. To the amazement of his friends, during the winter he booked into the exclusive Christ Hospital at Cincinnati for a three-week course of intensive therapy. In 1986 Steve became a tee-totaller and selective eater and has maintained his exceptional self-discipline ever since.

From 1985 to 1990 Steve was stable jockey to the nine-times Champion trainer, Henry Cecil, at Newmarket. Now he is retained by Sheikh Mohammed al Maktoum. His working year starts around 1 March. In the previous two months, he will have played golf in Barbados, soaked up the sun in Florida and played tennis with his mother Myra on the family farm at Walton, Kentucky. The first three weeks in Britain are spent riding out two lots of horses each day and evaluating the progress and potential of the stable's blue-blooded inmates. There is also the problem of whittling away the winter's surplus poundage.

'I still go running on the odd occasion, but not so often now. It builds up the muscles in your legs which is counter-productive. The next thing is you can't fit into your boots! I prefer to sweat – either in the sauna, with Walter Swinburn or Bruce Raymond – or in a hot bath, which I prefer. I can relax and read; have the telephone on hand, and lose 2 or 3lb in an hour and a quarter.

'On a normal day, I'll ride out first lot for Henry Cecil – which means there is no rush. Henry's string doesn't pull out until 8 a.m. Then it's back home to the telephone. I don't eat much breakfast … possibly a boiled egg if I feel like it. I'll call a few trainers; decide what horses I want to get on; talk to my agent John Hanmer; organise the travel plans; and co-ordinate the whole lot through my manager John Barnes.

'John has been with me for three years. He does my bookwork; public relations; handles the telephone; does the shopping; records the televised racing – and he's my driver. In fact, he's an invaluable right-hand man. He totally understands the game-plan. In this game, one phone call can mean that a whole week's plans can go down the tubes!

'The worst thing about our job is the travelling – it takes a helluva lot out of you – but luckily I find it easy to relax in a car. I'll either sleep, read the paper, or talk on the phone. I change my car every year, and comfort is a prime criterion.

'When we get to the races, I might have a cup of coffee or tea. I don't usually eat anything, but I might have a piece of fruit – something light. It's not very comfortable having food resting on your stomach. It's like giving a horse a sack of oats before he runs!

'I don't find racing physically tiring. Once you're fit for the season, you can ride all day. It's all the things that *surround* riding that create a mental fatigue. There's the Press, television, owners to talk to … it's all the ancillary things that make it a long day. As soon as I arrive, there are half a dozen people who want to talk. On some days I might need to lose half a pound in the sauna. Then you win a race and there's a television interview and the Press boys want a quote. It's a busy situation and it's mentally tiring. But I believe it has got to be done. My attitude is that every little item of promotion is helpful for racing so, within reason, I'm happy to do it.

'Of course, two meetings in one day, after a 5.30 start, can stretch you to the limit. You've got to pace yourself, or you end up crashed out. I like six to seven hours' sleep, and you've got to grab it when you can. You can't burn the candle at both ends.'

Steve, at 31, is already the weighing room's elder statesman. He has a good working relationship with the senior stewards' secretaries (whose job it is to advise the unpaid amateur local stewards), and he has been invited to collaborate on a teaching video for younger riders. 'It would be nice to say that every-

'That's the one I've got to beat.' Steve checks out the opposition in the *Racing Post*. Note the glass of iced Coke for brief sips pre-conversation, on a hot day.

Trainer Charlie Nelson unfastens the surcingle before fitting the visor, pulling back the rug, adjusting the girths and throwing the jockey into the saddle.

thing is sweetness and light between the jockeys and local stewards, but it is not. We feel that many of them are still living in the eighteenth century, and treat us like children. Mind you, sometimes they are right – some jockeys act like children! We just want to be treated like human beings and given a little respect.

'People complain about inconsistency in stewards' decisions, but with the British system it is inevitable. With 35 flat-race courses all with different sets of stewards, there are bound to be different verdicts. In America, there are professional stewards and you are riding at, say, Santa Anita six days a week, for

'The so-and-so's "gone".' Cauthen clenches his teeth as he returns to dismount. The filly finished 11th of 12.

four months. There's an understanding between the jockeys and stewards, and if you've got a bad feeling for someone, it is soon sorted out.'

The most contentious issue between stewards and jockeys in recent years has been the use of the whip. In America there are guidelines to whip technique, but no limit as to the extent of its use. The American approach to whip-riding was explained in Pete Axthelm's bestseller *The Kid*, which paid tribute to Steve's sensational season in 1977. It was the year that, at the age of 17, Steve rode 487 winners. The following year he rode the Triple Crown winner Affirmed. Affirmed's passage to the Kentucky Derby took in the Hollywood Derby. The colt's trainer, the late Laz Barrera, gave the following orders. 'I want you to send him to the front and keep him in the clear. Also, I think we've been babying him too much. Today, let him get used to being whipped.'

Axthelm writes:

> Cauthen followed the instructions with his usual precision. Setting a swift early pace, he raced the promising Radar Ahead into defeat, opened up a clear lead, and then began whipping. In all he hit his mount 12 times coming through the stretch. Beneath him Affirmed seemed to wonder what The Kid was getting so excited about ...

Such an episode would have caused horror in Britain and would certainly have led to a suspension for Steve. For a start, if a horse is hit more than ten times by a jockey, the stewards are obliged to consider holding an enquiry. 'It's a very sensitive area,' says Steve, 'and sometimes there is a lack of understanding. Ten is the number that someone thought up. But if you do the job with rhythm and finesse, 12 or 14 smacks can be quite acceptable. But another jockey could butcher a horse with 11 hits.

'Of course we have to live within guidelines and rules, but it's easy to see if someone is doing it properly or not. Pat Eddery, for instance, can be pretty tough on a horse, and you wouldn't always want to run a horse that Pat has ridden the following week. But he's doing it the right way. If you hit a horse in the wrong place – on the flank, for example – he doesn't go any faster. Quite the opposite – he resents it, and curls up. After you've hit a horse two or three times, you realise that either he's going to do his best, or, alternatively, that he doesn't like being hit. And that is one of the classic arts of jockeyship – knowing, sensing whether or not a horse is going to run for a smack.

'In some walks of life youth is a vital attribute. As you get older you become less effective. But jockeys get better with age. Experience is more important than brute strength. No jockey ever carried a horse past the post. Pat Eddery has a particular brand of genius. He's very strong, an effective whip-rider, and he has terrific balance. I like to think that I am equally effective in a different style, perhaps with more finesse and the ability to be in the right place at the right time. There are different ways to skin a cat!'

Many top flat-race jockeys, including Sir Gordon Richards and Lester Piggott, have continued to ride until their 50th year and beyond. No one expects Steve, with his wealth, his weight problems, and his broad appraisal of life, to follow this trail. But talk of his imminent retirement is premature. 'I feel

Jockey of the 1990s. Multi-millionaire Cauthen is, ironically, richer than 90 per cent of the owners he rides for. Gone are the days of the 'riding groom'. Brian Rouse looks on in envy.

Neck and neck. Four in a line at the finish of Newbury's straight mile. Jockeys enjoy riding at Newbury, one of Britain's fairest racecourses.

confident, and good, and I'm enjoying riding more than ever. Of course there are plenty of ups and downs, and no one gets more disappointed than a jockey when a horse that he expects to run well runs badly. But I've always believed in being positive. I'm a trier, and I have been all my life.

'Everyone in racing hits a bad run, and it's hard to handle. When you're winning everyone wants you, but when you're riding a lot of losers suddenly you're short of rides. It's easy to lose your confidence. You move a little too soon, or a little too late, on horses that *could* have won, and the pressure mounts. Of course everything is relative. If Pat goes three days without riding a winner everyone asks, "What's happening?" In the spring of 1977 in New York

'Has yours got a chance?' Ian Balding checks out Steve's opinion on a race in which Balding's runner is owned by The Queen. John Williams is the amused onlooker.

I was riding five or six winners a day. Two days running I didn't ride a winner, and I thought, "Christ!"'

It was on 23 May 1977 that Steve had his first bad fall. The horse he was riding snapped a leg, and went down. Two other horses crashed into horse and jockey. Steve was taken to hospital with a broken bone in his right arm; a fractured rib; two broken fingers; and severe concussion. Exactly a month later he was back in the saddle. His first ride back, Little Miracle, was a winner. It was his 277th of the year.

In August 1988 he suffered a considerably worse fall at Goodwood. He broke his neck, and was out of action for almost eight months. Many questioned whether he would ride again. The doubters' arguments were fuelled when in May 1990 Steve declined, at the eleventh hour, to ride a horse at Leicester, eight days before the Derby. Steve was fined £1000 for 'bringing racing into disrepute'. The episode still rankles. 'It wasn't the fall that made me make that decision. It was simply a matter of principle. I felt there were things about the horse that I should have been told before I was booked. I had to prove that I stand by what I believe.

'I've always known that falls are part of the game, and, yes, I do think about them sometimes. But you can't go out to ride if you're scared. A fall in a race is like an aeroplane crash – it's a million-to-one shot. I really don't feel any fear. *That* won't stop me riding. I'll carry on until I don't enjoy it enough to justify the sacrifices that I make.

'I'm lucky to ride horses that are good enough to win the big ones. That's what gives me a thrill. And sometimes there's just as much pleasure in winning a little race for a one-horse owner. That's a real buzz – giving something that not everyone could give. But there are lots of other things that I'd like to do in life. Above all, I'd like to go out at the top. If I can, I will.'

National Hunt

Introduction

Compared to the flat, National Hunt racing is a horse of a very different colour. Jumping is strictly for fun. There is no such thing as a million-pound jumper. No horse, however good, is worth more than his potential racecourse earnings. The reason is simple: 98 per cent of jumpers are either geldings or mares. Sadly, Arkle, Red Rum and Desert Orchid had their breeding potential removed at an early age. Ironically, the mare Dawn Run, the only horse to win the Champion Hurdle and Gold Cup who *could* have reproduced, was killed in a fall at Auteuil in France. So the individuals who own jumping horses do so purely for fun, and the thrill of competing.

Whereas flat racing is a major industry and the successful thoroughbred a valuable commodity to be protected, and inevitably retired to stud at the age of three, the jumping horse carries on as long as his legs will carry him. This factor has, in recent years, made National Hunt racing a considerably more popular television spectacle than flat racing. Viewers become attached to their favourites, and evergreens like Desert Orchid enjoy substantially more popularity than a Derby winner.

Jumping creates a wonderful bond between man and horse, and man and man. Jumping jockeys are the hardiest of breeds, seemingly impervious to pain and oblivious of danger. A special camaraderie exists which, in the eyes of many, makes them far more attractive as individuals than their wealthy flat-racing counterparts. Danger and death are never far distant and many jockeys are motivated as much by love of the sport as by potential profit. They are resigned to the inevitability of injury and pain and are stoical in their approach to the hazards of their chosen profession.

Jumping trainers, too, have a unique outlook. In recent years, the autumn months have been spent praying for rain and not daring to race or even gallop their horses on the persistently firm ground. No sooner does the rain arrive than it is followed by snow and a major freeze-up. By the time the ground thaws, the dry weather has returned and, hey presto, the season is over! Meanwhile, the long-suffering trainer has endured temperatures below freezing each morning; transported his horses many miles to gallop on the beach; spent hours rotovating land to create a galloping surface; and in the process broken down his best horse. While this is happening his second-best horse has been moved to Martin Pipe's stable, and his wife has run off to Barbados with a flat racing trainer.

All these hardships make jumping folk the most marvellous companions, and the most durable characters. Men like Josh Gifford, Toby Balding, Nick

'Aintree comes but once a year…' The field crashes through the Chair fence in the climax of
every jumping man's year, the Seagram Grand National.

Henderson and Jimmy Fitzgerald are not only marvellous hosts and hugely
entertaining people with whom to spend a day, they would also be fail-safe
comrades in the trenches.

If the finances of flat racing are cockeyed, the finances of jumping do not
bear discussion. But jumping people are disinclined to whinge. So long as
horse and jockey return in one piece, and the day has been fun, they are invariably content.

Jumping owners are normally countrymen, with either farming or live-
stock associations. Many keep their own horses, or at least hunters, at home,

and many either ride or have ridden themselves. They are resilient to the elements; feel undressed without a picnic basket and hip flask; and invariably get as close to the horses and action as logistics permit. They are jolly, companionable and caring. Jumping owners are divided as to whether they would rather win the Grand National or the Gold Cup. In recent years Cheltenham has gone from strength to strength, whilst Liverpool, despite a marked revival since the disaster years of the mid-1970s, still evokes mixed reactions as a result of the occasional widely chronicled fatality. Of course, there are business people, town dwellers and gamblers who own jumpers, but they are in a minority.

Gordon W. Richards is lucky to train for the best sportsmen, and he and Neale Doughty embrace all the best qualities of jumping men. Their stories are symptomatic of the winter game.

The Trainer

Gordon W. Richards

Gordon W. Richards is one of the elite band of horsemen to have trained more than one winner of the Grand National. He is very much a 'hands-on' trainer. At the age of 60 he rides out every morning when he is at home. He shrugs off discomfort from the broken back which ended his professional riding career and from the legacy of a major kidney operation two years ago.

'Pony-trekking' on a racing machine. Walking downhill helps a horse's balance and shoulder muscles.

Greystoke Castle, Penrith, home of the Howard family. 'G.W.' has trained at the Castle stables
for 24 years.

'This is the plan, boys.' Richards briefs his riding staff on the morning's work. Neale Doughty (fourth from left) has drawn the short straw.

One of ten children of a timber merchant from Bath, Avon, Richards's destiny was determined when his parents named him after the great Gordon. It was 1930, the year in which Gordon won his first Classics on Rose of England and Singapore, but lost the jockeys' title on the last day of the season to Freddie Fox. When the young Richards became apprentice to J. C. Waugh at Didcot, the 'W' was added to his name for convenience, to avoid professional confusion. His first job had been with the eccentric Mrs Louie Dingwell, who, in addition to her war effort activities, trained a few moderate horses – long before women were officially recognised – on the beach at Poole. His first ride was at a war-time meeting at Salisbury, aged 13. But before his 17th birthday he had switched to riding over hurdles and fences.

Now, in the post-war period, he moved to the great Ivor Anthony at Wroughton, near Swindon. Anthony had trained the evergreen Brown Jack, and the popular 1937 Grand National winner Royal Mail. Richards admired him immensely and to this day tries to do things in the way that Anthony would have done them. His ambitions as a jockey were slow to gather momentum. But like several flat-racing jockeys, notably Charlie Smirke and Ken

'Survival seat'. A Greystoke work-rider sits correctly with toes in and heels down, braced for a buck or any unexpected movement from a fresh horse.

'This might be a nice horse one day…' A typical backward, green G.W. chaser-type leads the string. The trainer has an exceptional knack of anticipating a horse's development.

The old stables were built by Joanie Richards's grandfather to accommodate his hunters. The grooms' bedrooms are overhead.

'Let's start at the beginning...' Richards launches some four-year-olds over poles in the
manège, to teach them the rudiments of jumping.

Gethin, he was also handy with his fists and won several amateur boxing
bouts. Occasionally, during hard times, he would moonlight in the fairground
boxing booths and 'earn a few quid for my supper!'

Eventually Ivor Anthony suggested that, with so many outstanding jockeys in the south, his career prospects would be enhanced in the north. 'G. W.'
accepted the position of stable jockey to Major Renwick, trainer at the private
stables of Mr John Marshall at Chatton Park, Northumberland. He has
remained an émigré from the south-west ever since. 'All I would say about
Gordon's career as a jockey is that it's lucky he is a better trainer than he was a
jockey – considerably better!' recollects former top northern jockey, now starter, Gerry Scott. 'Admittedly he did not have the best of horses to ride, but you
could not say that he set the game alight.'

Richards married his first wife, Jean Charlton, the daughter of a well-to-do
Northumbrian farmer, in 1955. His riding career was never spectacular, but it
came to an abrupt halt at Perth in 1959. His back injuries were so severe that

Greystoke offers the seclusion of private land and a variety of routes to the exercise grounds.

retirement was inevitable. 'It was a bad time,' he reflects. 'I was married with a young son and I couldn't work for six months. It was a struggle. I was never without an overdraft. I would buy horses and sell them on. I "made" hunters and during the summer I would run a riding school to get a few quid together. The first horse that I bought could have finished me!

'The trainer I was riding for when I broke my back rang me up and invited me to tea. "I've got a horse that might suit you," he said. We had our tea – it was a grand tea – and off we went to a nearby farm. There were six horses there, but there was only one he wanted to show me. "Would you like a sit on?" he asked. I answered, "Yes, I would." So he said to the lad: "Go and get a saddle." The lad replied: "We've only got two saddles, and they're both being mended."

'"Ride him bareback, Gordon," said my host. "Not likely," I replied. "Quite right … no need … take the horse," he said. "Look at him … grand horse … take him home." So I bought the horse for £400, and turned him away. But one thing worried me – people kept on asking me if I'd ridden him yet.

'Eventually I could stand it no longer. I threw a saddle on him, jumped up – and splonk. I was flat on my back! The second time I just stayed on, but Lord knows how. So I took him to the beach to give him some work. That went reasonably well, but at the end I couldn't dismount! Finally I backed him into a barn, and slid off.

'I could write a book about the next few months, but eventually we mastered him, and he actually won a race. And there he was – the man who sold him to me. "Ah, young Gordon – I *knew* you were the man for that horse," he said!'

Ironically, the first horse that Richards trained turned out to be one of the very best. Playlord was an unbroken two-year-old when G. W. first set eyes on him. He was owned by a farmer friend called Adam Pringle. Pringle persuaded Richards to take out a licence and he started with Playlord and just two other horses on the beach at Chathill, near Alnwick. Within days of Playlord coming up for his first race, Adam Pringle died. Richards was doubly distraught. He had lost a friend and the executors wanted to sell Playlord. Richards was determined to have him and asked the bank manager for an overdraft to buy him. He was curtly refused. As a last resort, Jean Richards borrowed £1400 from an aunt. Playlord was theirs. After an educational outing, Playlord won his next three races and Gordon Richards never looked back.

Clean winds and strong muscles are just two of the rewards of cantering work on the Cumbrian fells. And there are the spectacular views!

A healthy horse drinks two buckets (six gallons) of water a day.

The work is done and it's time for a pick of grass. One horse is being dried off, while his companions get their heads down.

The woodchip all-weather gallop is chain harrowed daily. Richards has remarkable success with the few flat-race horses that he trains.

'His first win was at Bogside – the last meeting they ever had there. Jumbo Wilkinson rode him. He was just about to retire, but I rang him up and said: "Hang on Jumbo, I might just have a *racehorse* for you to ride ..."' Over the following season Playlord, now owned by the wealthy industrialist Phillip Cussins, won a further nine races including the Great Yorkshire Chase and Scottish Grand National. Gordon Richards, trainer, was on his way. Titus Oates, Lucius and Sea Pigeon (Richards 'made' him before he departed to Peter Easterby) followed on.

Richards moved, as a tenant, to Greystoke Castle, near Penrith, in March 1967, three years after his first licence. He has trained at Greystoke ever since, and will end his days there. Sadly, his devoted and hard-working first wife Jean died in 1978, after surviving several earlier coronaries. In 1980, Richards married divorcee Joanie Dacre, a member of the Howard family, who own Greystoke Castle and its 4000 acre estate. The present occupant is Neville Howard.

A jumping lesson over tyres: an intermediary stage for young jumpers. They are inviting, but solid – note the pole supporting the tyres.

It was Joanie's grandfather who built the stable block that houses Richards's steeplechasers. The outside stonework is designed in an 'H H H' motif, informing the gods, and lesser mortals, that these were Henry Howard's Hunters. G. W. and Joanie live at The Old Rectory, Greystoke, less than a quarter of a mile from the castle. 'I'm a lucky man to have had two wonderful women in my life,' he reflects.

The element that sets Richards aside from many of his competitors is the type of horse in his stable. He favours the strong, robust steeplechaser type of horse, rather than the former flat racing type. He buys almost all of the horses he trains at the sales at Doncaster, and at Fairyhouse in Ireland. 'I buy some as foals, some as yearlings, and some as three-year-olds. The Edinburgh Wool Company's [his main patron] horses are all bought in Ireland, at auction. They're all lovely horses.

'I've been very lucky buying foals. We bring them back here, castrate them as yearlings in August or September, and run them out and in. We don't leave

Schooling at Greystoke. The portable fences can be moved to a fresh site when the ground becomes churned on the landing or take-off side.

them out in the winter ... up here we're not lucky enough with the weather. I've put up a big shed with a woodchip area for them to run about on during the bad weather. There's an outside arena on both sides of the shed, for cattle on one side and horses on the other. It covers an acre in all.

'I usually have 30 or 40 babies on the place. Some are passed on to our clients. If they don't come up to scratch we send them to the sales.'

Years of training success have enabled Richards to accumulate valuable land. He has a farm of 110 acres acquired gradually since 1976 and managed by his son Nicky. He also owns 22 acres of land at nearby Motherby as an over-flow area for young stock.

For many years his mentor in the sale rings of Ireland was the legendary bloodstock agent Jack White. It was White who, more recently, helped to nurture the talents of racing's number one pinhooker, Timmy Hyde. (A pin-hooker is an individual who buys foals to re-sell ten months later as yearlings.)

'To begin with I would rarely buy a horse without asking his opinion. The other day Jack said to me, "Gordon, you're better than me now!" I don't know about that. We're a company, but he's the boss!'

Richards has the elusive knack of anticipating a young horse's development. 'I try to think how a horse might grow, how he might finish up. I'll study his length of leg. It's not easy to put into words. It's something you've either got the gift of, or not. Buying a three-year-old is a shade easier. It's still an immature horse, but now there's a frame, and everything is there.

Boxes that were built to last. A typical G.W. chaser-type is brushed and groomed in a traditional box, with contemporary paper bedding underfoot.

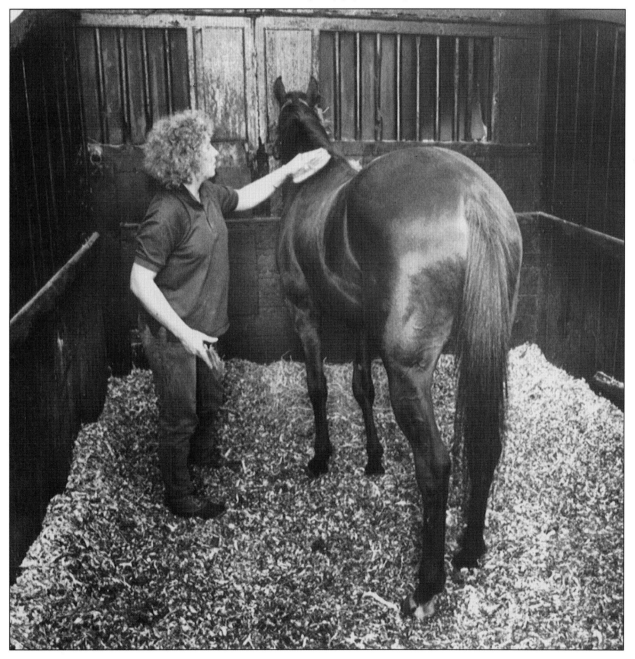

At 60, Richards remains very much a 'hands-on' trainer. When he is at home he rides out every morning.

G.W. uses the manège as a loose school for beginners. Never over-faced, young horses look forward to their jumping sessions.

'It's always the *horse* that I look at first, rather than the pedigree. Of course, pedigree does help if you're buying for a businessman. They can read, and they like to see a bit of black type. But I'm buying to win races, so it doesn't matter a lot to me. If you do take pedigree into account, I feel the dam's side is more important than the sire's.

Richards's rest home: the specially-designed open barn for horses maturing, convalescing, and roughed off. At the end of the barn is an all-weather arena where horses are turned out for two or three hours a day.

'We start on the young horses as three-year-olds. We get them broken in, and give them a bit of work. I like to kick them in the belly, and teach them something. Then we finish with them, and leave them alone for six to nine months. The following spring we ease them into work for a couple of months of education. We school them over some logs to teach them the rudiments of jumping, and then chuck them away again.

Jumping horses are often shod with light steel racing plates which are more resilient than the aluminium plates fitted to flat-race horses.

Joanie Richards with friends. Joanie works as secretary, telephonist, press liaison officer, and chief cook. 'I'm lucky to have had two wonderful women in my life,' says G.W.

The road home. Neale Doughty leads the group of 'schoolers' back to the yard.

'Watch the birdie!' Scottish Grand National winner Four Trix is singularly unimpressed by efforts to make him stand correctly.

As the Richards Grand National runners reach the security of the racecourse stables, above lies a stark reminder of the hazards of Aintree.

'I feel you haven't got a *proper* jumping horse until he is five. In fact, I've got plenty of six-year-olds here who have only had one run in their life. With National Hunt horses you've got to be patient … it pays in the end. Everyone who joins me as an owner understands that. Some people like to run young horses in "bumpers" [National Hunt flat races], but I'm not so keen on them. You've got to gee them up a bit to compete.

'The earliest I like to run a horse is at four years, but preferably at five. I run them when they are starting to tell me something. Usually in the spring I've got a dozen horses that I *should* give a run to, but if the ground is firm I'll probably rough them off. But it does help to lob them round as an education. You always hope that a young horse is going to be something special, but you don't really know until you work them.

'It's the top bracket that you're after. Everything I buy is the chasing type. I don't really like buying hurdle-type horses off the flat.'

Patience is a virtue that has paid off for Gordon Richards. It has kept him at the top of a ruthlessly competitive profession for over 20 years. As well as his two Grand Nationals, he has won a King George VI Chase; a Whitbread Gold Cup; a Mackeson Gold Cup; and a Scottish Grand National. 'Racing has been

The trappings of success. G.W.'s racing achievements have made him a man of considerable
property. Home is The Old Rectory, Greystoke.

my life – and it's a great life, but I've worked hard at it. When I started off I had nothing. It has been very pleasing to build things up little by little. Two years ago when I had my kidney operation I thought that I wouldn't be able to train. I was really, really down. But even now, I'm enjoying my racing although, with the pain from my back, I need a bit of support after a long day.

'I hope to go on for another four or five years. My son Nicky would like to train, but he's more interested in the flat. If I do retire, I'll always have horses around … the odd point-to-pointer perhaps. I would always have a nice horse.

'I've met a lot of nice people over the years. A lot of my owners are far more than that – they are good friends. People like the Whittakers [the owners of Lucius] … Fiona Whittaker is more like a sister. Of course you meet some bad people as well.

'Above all, I've always tried to do the job like a true professional, the way that Ivor Anthony would have done it.'

The Jump Jockey

Neale Doughty

Neale Doughty's racing year begins around mid-July. He will arrive at Gordon W. Richards's Greystoke Stables on a Monday morning to begin the long build-up for horse and jockey to the new season. His weight will be between 11st and 11st 7lb after the excesses of the early summer. By the time he weighs out for his first ride of the new season he will have shed over a stone.

The National Hunt season runs relentlessly from the first week of August to the first week of June. During that period the top riders will have up to 600 rides, covering around 1500 miles over obstacles of varying sizes and durability. The jockey's fee for each of these rides is £71.50 plus VAT. Occasionally a jockey would gladly donate his fee for the pleasure of riding a particular horse. In other cases double the fee is scant reward for the risk to life and limb.

Back to work. Both horse and jockey will be overweight after the summer break. But it's good to be back…

Hard work on the hill. The Cumbrian fells provide the perfect stage for conditioning work for burly, overweight horses.

Doughty is one of the lucky ones. Riding for Gordon W. Richards is a prestigious and privileged job. 'Even schooling is a pleasure at Greystoke,' he smiles. 'If a horse won't jump for G. W. he won't jump for anyone. I can't remember ever having a schooling fall. He's a great man to ride for. He will never ask you to do anything that he would not do himself.'

Greystoke Stables in July is like a seaside resort during winter. The yard is deserted except for a handful of horses that have been running on the flat. The remainder will be scattered around sleepy green fields, enjoying their summer break and clearing their digestive systems with the aid of Dr Grass. Gordon W. Richards has over 100 acres of paddocks close to his home, where the majority of his horses spend their break. The others will return home to owners, whose

The schooling lane. Solid telegraph poles prevent young horses from developing sloppy habits.

Blue skies … long grass … a perfect early autumn morning. The 'early ones' are starting to move into gear.

pleasure in ownership is enhanced by day-to-day acquaintance with their pride and joy. It is this personal and lasting relationship with jumping horses that makes their occasional tragic demise so hard to bear.

Richards goes round his fields twice a day to check the horses. Gradually, towards the beginning of August, they will be fed back into the system. 'They start off with roadwork to harden them up,' says Neale. 'Then the "early" runners will start cantering, probably on the all-weather gallop. The "early" ones won't have been let down for so long. That makes it easier to get them fit. Most of the horses won't start racing again until October or November. We don't have many firm-ground horses. The early autumn racing suits horses from the flat. From a jockey's point of view, to get race-riding fit you've got to ride in races. You can run and swim and that takes you to a certain stage, but it's only race-riding that makes everything work.'

In 1988 Doughty ignored the autumn racing and spent the time building a house. Normally, after a few freelance rides in August and September, his season moves into top gear as the better horses appear for the big Wetherby October meeting and the Mackeson meeting at Cheltenham. His day begins at 6.30. He will wash, shave, and collect the morning papers from Penrith, two or three miles away. After a quick read and a cup of tea, he will drive to Greystoke for first lot at 7.45. On a quiet day he will ride just one horse, perhaps changing briefly onto two or three others if they need to be 'blown out'. On

Walking home. Girths are loosened and horses relax after a rigorous cantering and schooling session.

Battle of the scales. It's Stratford on 8 September and 12st 3lb is a convenient weight after the summer break. Declan Murphy waits his turn.

work days (Wednesday and Saturday), he might ride eight to ten horses, probably over seven furlongs or a mile on the grass. On a schooling day Doughty will also ride several horses. Greystoke has a 'jumping lane' with several flights of hurdles and three portable fences which can be moved when the ground becomes churned up on the take-off side.

After first lot, Doughty will return for a coffee to G. W.'s house and ride out second lot if he is not racing. Otherwise, he returns straight home – if there's time – to change for the races. 'It's a great place to live for the northern meetings,' Doughty enthuses. 'Nowhere is more than two hours away and Haydock is only one hour. The A1 and the M6 serve us well.

Ring of confidence. Pinemartin, Doughty's mount in the novices' chase, is a 7–4 shot after winning twice at Cartmel. The relaxed owner is Jim Martin, with fellow owner Gill Jones.

Stratford, sited a mile southwest of the tourist town, always attracts good sporting crowds –
many from the Birmingham area.

'I certainly have to watch my weight. During the season I have no breakfast as such, and no lunch. I don't eat until after I have finished riding, then I'll have a sandwich and a cup of tea in the weighing room. Racing finishes early in the winter, and I'll have my evening meal between 7 and 7.30. I'll have either steak, fish or chicken, with a vegetable or perhaps a salad, and occasionally the odd glass of wine. Afterwards, I'll relax or ring up G. W. to discuss how the horses ran. I'll watch the Nine O'Clock News and go to bed at 10.

'G. W. and I spend a lot of time on the phone. We have a lot of novices and we'll talk at length discussing their future, whether they are ready to go on, or if they need another year. We don't have flat racing types at all. Our horses are all potential chasers. When Graham McCourt comes here to ride out he finds it hard to adjust. His main job is for Nigel Tinkler, who buys nearly all of his horses off the flat. He says ours are another species and feel completely different!'

Ea-sy! Pinemartin completes his hat-trick by two lengths. It was the first leg of a treble for Doughty.

Because of the quality horses that he rides, Doughty has been luckier than many with falls. 'I've had a few knocks. Three seasons ago at Sedgefield I had my worst accident. I was riding a finish on the run-in when a loose horse came straight at me, galloping the wrong way round the track. We hit head-on and both horses were killed. I crushed two vertebrae and had multiple fractures of three ribs. You often sense when something's gone wrong and when something is going to happen. In a case like that, it's just a matter of praying. I didn't ride at Sedgefield for the next two seasons. In fact, we have very few runners there – our type of horse isn't suited to the sharp, undulating track.'

In an age when the majority of top National Hunt jockeys – notably Dunwoody and Scudamore – are former amateurs, Doughty is professional through and through. He was born in the Rhondda district of South Wales, at Kenfig Hill, Mid Glamorgan, deep in rugby country and just seven miles from the steel works at Port Talbot. His father was a steel worker and his mother was

Doughty rides Full Strength in the day's top race. 1990–91 was Doughty's best ever season
and at one stage during the autumn he was top jockey.

Full Strength arches his back in the classic style as he flies the water. The handsome seven-year-old won ten races in a row before being killed in a fall at Ascot.

'It was easy, Sir – he's a star.' Doughty is debriefed by owner John Moreton (left).

Sheer delight! A thoroughbred enjoys nothing more than a roll in the sand to relax and ease out irritations and saddle marks.

a daughter of the valleys. The Doughtys are a sporting family. Neale's sister Julie played hockey for Wales at both schoolgirl and national level, and was ladies' tennis champion of Glamorgan. Neale himself was a useful centre three-quarter for his school rugby XV, in a side that boasted future internationals Ray Giles and Alan Phillips. But it was horses that always attracted him.

'My parents scrimped and saved to buy me a small mountain pony. We built a horsebox out of a caravan chassis and I went round the shows. Eventually, I outgrew my pony so we sold him and the horsebox. With the money, we bought a new pony ... and built a new box! Everyone said that I'd be a jockey, but I was worried that I would grow too big. I was supposed to sit my O Levels, but I wrote to Fulke Walwyn and asked for a job. He replied "Come and see me at the Welsh Champion Hurdle meeting." I met him – and I started work a week later.' Doughty stayed with Walwyn for a year, and learnt the all-important rudiments of stablecraft. 'When you learn the job in our yard,' said head lad Darkie Deacon, 'you learn it the proper way.' Doughty learned how horses were fed, trained and groomed. But he realised that if he remained at Walwyn's he would be a small cog in a big wheel.

A special friend. Neale has a high regard for Nickle Silver. The American head-gear is the
legacy of a working visit to Neil Drysdale's barn at Hollywood Park.

He left after a year, with a view to returning to school to acquire some qualifications. But barely had he returned home when a friend passed on the offer of a job with the former Scottish rugby international Wilf Crawford, now a trainer at Haddington, East Lothian, in Scotland. Doughty went north … and stayed for three years. They were happy years. Ron Barry was there when he first arrived from Ireland. 'I rode my first winner there, at Perth in September 1977 and was on my way.'

During the summer of 1978, Doughty moved south to spend a 'holiday' riding flat-race horses for Bill Marshall at Newmarket. 'I thought it would be useful experience and would make me tidier,' he reflects. As the autumn approached, the head lad, Andy Boult, mentioned that the stable would have a dozen jumpers in training that winter. On the same day, Doughty asked Bill Marshall if he would apply for a licence on his behalf. 'How can I get you a licence when I haven't seen you ride?' exploded the irascible Marshall.

The following morning Doughty schooled six or eight horses for Marshall with Scobie Coogan, a local freelance, on the Links Training Ground. 'I got back to the yard and the head lad came straight over; "The boss wants to see you in his office." I thought my career with Bill Marshall had started and finished in one morning. Bill Marshall stood there with tears in his eyes. He shook my hand and said: "Son, I haven't had a kid like you since Ron Atkins and Bill Smith." He got my licence by special courier, and off we went in the horsebox to Newton Abbot for the first meeting of the season. I slept in the wagon with the lads. I had no rides on the first day, but had two on the Monday.'

In the last race, the heavy-betting Marshall saddled two runners, Neronian, the 15–8 favourite ridden by Bill Smith, and Temoke ridden by Doughty. 'His orders were: "Go out and enjoy yourself, and do your best." I won by three parts of a length, hands and heels from Neronian,' Doughty recollects. 'Afterwards, Bill Marshall gathered Bill Smith, Ron Atkins and me together and said: "Boys, I've done it again … I've done my brains! But at least I've got a kid who can ride winners!" He was like a father to me. He kept telling me I could ride when I didn't really believe it. I rode a dozen winners that season, including the Daily Express Triumph Hurdle Trial on Alaskan Prince at 33–1.'

Fate took a hand halfway through Doughty's second season with the volatile Marshall. One day at the races, Gordon W. Richards asked Wilf Crawford if he had seen any good lads riding recently. 'I know of one lad,' replied Crawford, 'but he's gone to Bill Marshall.' Doughty reflects: 'G.W. saw me riding at Warwick one day, tapped Bill Marshall on the shoulder, and the rest is history.'

The association between Richards and Doughty has lasted – with occasional turbulence – for 11 years. 'I was a bit concerned when I went to Greystoke. I had to confess to the boss that I had only had two rides over fences – both times on a four-year-old – and had fallen at the first fence both times! "Don't worry lad," he replied. "Jonjo [O'Neill] was the same when he came off the boat. It's just a question of practice." My first season was hard, but

I enjoyed my second year because I was more sure of myself, and because of the number of steeplechasers that I rode. I rode 21 winners and 17 of them were in steeplechases. Riding over fences is much more skilful. You go steadier, and you can't get away with things that you can over hurdles.

'We've had our ups and downs, the boss and me, but we know each other better than anyone now. He's a great man to train a Grand National horse and that's the race of all races for me.

'I hope to ride for two or three more years, and then I would like to assist the boss. I like living in the north-west. It's my home now, and I love it. It's near enough God's country. It's been good to me.'